He Cares for Me is a li... spiritual and emotional freedom. Drawing on years of applying Biblical truth in her own life, and ministering that truth with compassion to others, Marlene offers hope for those yearning to walk in victory. This book also contains practical and insightful principles for every believer who desires to be an instrument God can use to minister healing to the hurting as well!

> *Jodie Chiricosta*
> *Vice President*
> *Somebody Cares America/International*
> *"A True Witness Rescues Lives" Prov. 14:25*
> *www.somebodycares.org*

Pastor Marlene Yeo is an advocate to the broken and distressed people helping them to find healing and wholeness through the power of Jesus Christ. *"He Cares for Me"* is a comprehensive book which instructs readers that there is no level of bondage, brokenness, or depravity too powerful for God. Yeo's personal journey to healing and wholeness through tears, pain, and faith is woven throughout the book, making it both personal and relatable. Each chapter encourages people to begin their recovery in Christ by identifying the issues of life and implementing methods of recovery, supported strongly with Scripture. Anyone who is sincerely seeking wholeness and healing should read *He Cares for Me.*

> *David Hanshumaker*
> *Associate Pastor*
> *Community Christian Fellowship*
> *Haverhill, Ma*

He Cares For Me provides living proof that Jesus came to bind up the brokenhearted and set the captives free.

i

He Cares For Me

Through personal testimonies and simple principles, *He Cares for Me* boldly proclaims that there is an answer to our brokenness, there is healing, there is deliverance. For everyone who longs for wholeness, this book provides a deeper understanding of what it really means to have Jesus bear our sins and sorrows, and how the church can bring this hope to the world.

Kate Bailey
MPH
Haverhill, Massachusetts

I have known Pastor Marlene Yeo for more than 12 years, as her Pastor and comrade in the faith. Anyone familiar with Pastor Marlene has witnessed her relentless passion for God and sincere compassion for people. As a woman familiar with pain and struggle, her passion for God and compassion for people were ignited when she encountered, first hand, the great love of our Father God.

He Cares For Me is not another litany of well-meaning, but futile steps to wholeness. But rather *He Cares For Me* is a proven methodology of biblically based promises that deliver. I have personally known individuals who have been through the *He Cares For Me* ministry; they experienced glorious salvation, healing, and deliverance.

We are created in the image of God. As a triune God, we are triune beings consisting of spirit, soul and body. Our spirits can become born again, but our souls are in need of restoration. Through the liberating love of the Father who cares for us, this book has the capacity to restore your soul.

"The Lord is my shepherd; I shall not want. He makes me to lie down in green pastures; He leads me beside the

Endorsements

still waters. He restores my soul: He leads me in the paths of righteousness for His name's sake."

Psalm 23:1-3

Apostle Rafael Najem
Community Christian Fellowship Ministries
105 Princeton BLVD
Lowell, MA

There is such a need in the church today to understand the ministry of healing and deliverance. Though we know that God loves the broken hearted, and doesn't want them to remain broken, few seem to be doing something about it. *He Cares for Me* is a must for those who care about what God cares about.

Melinda and I have been involved with counseling and deliverance ministries for many years and have learned many valuable lessons. We know of no book that better pulls all these together in such a beautiful way, while presenting some new thoughts that help minister to others.

As Pastor's we see people who struggle with the same issues over and over again. We know from Scripture, if you don't get the root you will continue to get the fruit, and that is precisely the issue–getting to the root! *He Cares for Me* reveals the Father's desire for us to deal with the root issues that have allowed the enemy a place which steals the victory that Christ has already provided for them. Healing Waters weekend will change any believer's life. Melinda and I have personally seen the results and are using the model of *He Cares for Me* in our own church.

We have known Marlene Yeo for many years and have watched her journey in helping others. She is relentless in her pursuit of helping people find true and lasting freedom. She is an amazing, selfless and beautiful example of Christ! We cannot more highly endorse or recommend this book to you.

Chad and Melinda Waller
Lead Pastors VC2 Tennille, Georgia
WHP Founders and Directors

This book reveals the Heart of God that is in Marlene Yeo. She has God's heart for the world, for hurting people and to see marriages strengthened. I have known Marlene since 2004 and have seen her ministry in action pouring out God's love and care.

Melvin Adams
Evangelist
Former Harlem Globetrotter
Tomball, TX
http://adamsentertainmentagency.com

The message of hope and healing is skillfully written with a rare mix of love and practical wisdom. A compassionate spiritual harvest of redemptive insights that will both excite and challenge the reader. Pastor Marlene not only put words together with a warm and glowing heart, but she practically lives it. She is a completely sold out woman of God who is worthy following as she continues to live and follow the example of Christ.

I will gladly share this book with many of my personal and professional friends. I feel honored to be a comrade in the gospel with Pastor Marlene Yeo.

Endorsements

May you continue this road as He who began a good work in you carries it to completion.

Nomsa Ncube, MPS
JFK School of Government
Harvard University
Director of Projects

I have often wondered the source of Marlene's joy. Katy and I have been blessed for more 15 years to be around her on mountain tops, in the valley and everything in between. No matter where she finds herself there is joy, an unspeakable joy.

Our life is the result of choices. Our choices are rooted in our beliefs of who we are and where our identity lies. If our identity is in anything other than Christ we are lost. It is easy to say, but Marlene and the insights she shares in this book is the IDENTITY handbook.

Marlene Yeo is someone who lives in this reality and continues to give her life to anyone who wants to walk in the same reality.

Read this book. Do what it says to do. She sure is smart for making it so simple. Get ready to watch your life become an encounter with the living and loving Father.

Pastor Matt and Katy Stevens
Somebody Cares Baltimore
Founders and Directors

In her book *He Cares for Me*, Marlene communicates eloquently the heart of God in a captivating way - something she's demonstrated throughout her life to many people. I am sure this book will lead each reader into a deeper, richer relationship with Jesus.

Pastor Jude Fouquier
Lead Pastor
The City Church
Ventura, California

I read the manuscript in one setting, drawn from one chapter to the next, with vocal expressions of praise for the testimonies etching my heart and mind. In our 30 plus years of Pastoral ministry, never have we seen so many tools in application of Word and Spirit presented in a single volume. The burden of healing spirit, soul and body has become a Bethesda moment. In the telos of God, you'll bless the day you read and embraced these transformational truths.

Pastors Daniel and Cindy Wermuth
Joplin Family Worship Center

He Cares
For Me

Marlene J. Yeo

Additional materials cited:
Hartman, T. (1998). The Color Code: a new way to see yourself, your relationships, and life. New York, NY: Simon & Schuster.

Rogers, A., & Rogers, S. (2014). Unveiling the End Times in Our Time The Triumph of the Lamb in Revelation. Nashville, TN: B & H Publishing Group.

Warner, M., & Wilder, E. J. (2016). Rare leadership: 4 uncommon habits for increasing trust, joy, and engagement in the people you lead. Chicago, IL: Moody.

Arnott, J. (1977). What Christians should know about ... the importance of forgiveness. Kent, England: Sovereign World.

http://en.wikipedia.org/wiki/Brain
http://en.wikipedia.org/wiki/Sleep_cycle
http://www.glowtorch.org

Stringer, D. (2016). Leadership awakening: foundational principles for lasting success. New Kensington, PA: Whitaker House. (Page 83)

Contact Information:

Waller-Hill Publishing
P.O. Box 493
Tennille, GA 31089
wallerhill.com

10 9 8 7 6 5 4 3 2 1

This book is dedicated to:

All the broken, hurt people who need to know there is a God who is their Father, who sent His Son Jesus, suffered, and died for them. He Cares for Me and you, and desires for us to receive His love and forgiveness. Jesus came to reveal the Father's love, to give us salvation, healing and deliverance and a future and a hope! Don't delay any longer! Receive His gift of love and live life to the fullest, as it is meant to be, in the righteousness, joy, love, peace and in the power of the Holy Spirit!

Table Of Contents

Foreword

There may come moments in life when we may wonder, "Who Cares?" or think to ourselves, "no one cares" for me. King David himself even contemplated thoughts like these when he was seeking refuge in the cave of Adullam, stating, "No one cares for my soul".

If you spend any length of time around Marlene Yeo, you quickly become aware of how much she cares. Her passion for God is contagious and her compassion for people, many of whom others may have already given up on, is obvious.

I've known Marlene for nearly over 15 years. Time has proven the consistency of her pursuit of God's Presence and the heart to express Him in very tangible ways. She is not only a uniquely gifted communicator and passionate individual, her love and compassion for people attracts attention from God and is contagious to those who have the pleasure of being around her.

Reading through her latest book, *He Cares For Me*, you will not only find yourself encouraged and empowered in your own walk, but also equipped to bring a message of hope and healing to others.

The book is filled with testimonies and practical pathways that can help to shed light on areas that have been obstacles to finding freedom and liberty in your life and to those you care about. It is refreshing to see it's not necessarily a theological or theoretical treatise, yet it is filled with scripture, biblical principles and practical examples.

One of the ways to liberty and freedom is to have a love for truth. With honest candor, Marlene has an ability to speak the truth in love, yet seasoned with great grace. I trust that those who prayerfully and honestly seek the Lord as you read through this book, will find significant new ways He will work in and through your life.

Doug Stringer
Founder / President
Somebody Cares America
Somebody Cares International
Houston, Texas

Preface

I was born in 1952 to alcoholic parents, and raised in a typical American Christian home. My family attended church on the expected holidays of Easter and Christmas. My parents were hard workers who did the best they knew how with what they had. I was never given a moral or spiritual compass to navigate the challenges of my childhood, teenage, or young adult years.

I don't remember even once having a meaningful conversation with my parents about life, God, sexuality, marriage, heartache or brokenness. I had absolutely no idea what life was all about or what my purpose was, that is until I met Jesus at 26 years old.

I married my high school sweetie, football captain Harry Yeo at age of 18, just five months after graduating high school. After several years of living hand to mouth and partying on the weekends I felt an empty void and wanted something more in life.

Thinking that a baby would fill that void, we had our first son, Brandon, who was born four years after we married. Fifteen years later, prophets Steve and Rita Fidele ministered to our family and the word of the Lord spoken over Brandon was,

"I see you about four years old crying out to the Lord, 'I want a mommy and a daddy, I want love.' It was then I [The Lord] heard your cry, son, and I did visit your house with salvation."

In January 1977, one month before Brandon turned four, I met Jesus Christ as my personal Lord and Savior. I know my salvation experience was directly related to my son crying out to God for love. I know and I am persuaded that God hears the cries of His children.

Until meeting Christ, I modeled the same parenting skills as my parents. Although I wanted to do better, there was a wounded child within me who needed healing. I couldn't give my child what he needed most: a mature, sacrificial love that was able to provide a sense of identity, stability, and guidance.

Two more children were added to our family. Bethany was born in December of 1977, and Aaron was born in October of 1982. God has used my children to reveal the Father's love and to confront the areas of brokenness from my own childhood. Since having received Jesus as my Savior and experienced His forgiveness, the Holy Spirit has been teaching, training and perfecting me as a parent, leader and now a grandparent because Children are a gift from the Lord they are a reward from Him. *(Psalm 127:3 NIV)*

Psalm 138:6-8 says,

"Though the LORD is on high,
Yet He regards the lowly;
But the proud He knows from afar.
Though I walk in the midst of trouble,
You will revive me;
You will stretch out Your hand Against the wrath of my enemies,

And Your right hand will save me.
The LORD will perfect that which concerns me;
Your mercy, O LORD, endures forever;
Do not forsake the works of Your hands."

He is the One who forms the human heart in the womb, and He is the only One who can transform it. I once heard someone say, "The issue of the heart is the heart of the issue." As I have personally experienced the power of the Holy Spirit, and deliverance from the strongholds of sin, my parenting, thus my pastoring, has changed.

I have learned from my Teacher that His ways are higher than mine. He doesn't just deal with our bad behavior, He deals with the brokenness at the root of the bad behavior. He is focused on the why we do what we do, not simply on what we do. Most disciplinary methods only deal with behavior modification through suffering, painful consequences or medication to suppress negative behaviors.

Since 1986, I have served in the local church as a ministry leader, youth pastor, associate pastor and since 2005, lead pastor. I have found discipleship and parenting consist of the same components. There is a lack of understanding of true discipleship among the church community of believers. A parallel can be found between the break down in the family in America as well as family in church culture. There is a lack of love, respect, nurture and biblical discipline. The saying goes, "As it is in the family, it is in the church" and "As goes the church, so goes the nation." It is very easy to see the brokenness in individuals in the church body as they act out mindsets, manners, and methods they live out in their interpersonal lives within the home.

Just because someone accepts Christ as Lord and Savior doesn't automatically guarantee healing of their wounded soul. Healing is a lifetime journey that is only possible when an individual invites the Holy Spirit to shine His light in the dark recesses of deep emotional wounds and unhealthy mindsets. We must be willing to humble ourselves, repent, ask for forgiveness, give forgiveness, and obey the Word of God to bless, not curse, those who wounded our souls or caused us sorrow.

Who Cares For My Soul?

This book is about how very much Jesus cares for me and you. You will read several testimonies from real people about the freedom they have found in Christ, and how they have grown and matured as individuals and leaders. I pray that you will glean wisdom, gain insight, be encouraged and find hope through the testimonies shared. As we humble ourselves and invite the Lord into our broken messed up lives, He makes something beautiful and brings a message of hope through us to the world. As it says in Ecclesiastes 3:11 *"He has made everything beautiful in its time..."*

For believers, there is only one way to find and experience healing for our souls that we all long for. It is found in our faith in Christ and the finished work of the cross. Before healing can happen we must deal with the double mindedness that keeps us in the valley of decision, vacillating between two opinions. Joshua exhorted the people to make up their minds in Joshua 24:14-15:

> *"Now therefore, fear the LORD, serve Him in sincerity and in truth, and put away the gods which your fathers served on the other side of the River and in Egypt. Serve the LORD! And if it seems evil to you to serve the LORD, choose for yourselves this day whom you will serve, whether the gods which your fathers served that were on the other side of the River, or the gods of the Amorites, in whose land you dwell. But as for me and my house, we will serve the LORD."*

Are you going to serve the gods of your father that have been controlling and tormenting your family bloodline for generations? Are you going to serve the gods of culture that have come to twist your heart and mind with the intent to possess your soul to worship self with all of its perversion and filth? James 1:7-8 says:

"For let not that man suppose that he will receive anything from the Lord; he is a double-minded man, unstable in all his ways."

James uses a word to describe this condition that translates "double-minded," but the Greek word dipsuchos enlarges the meaning to include double-souled, or split-souled, or the un-centered soul. Jesus needs to be the center of our souls because disconnected souls live a vulnerable life. A soul without Jesus at the center has difficulty making decisions. James 1:5-6 says:

"If any of you lacks wisdom, let him ask of God, who gives to all liberally and without reproach, and it will be given to him. But let him ask in faith, with no doubting, for he who doubts is like a wave of the sea driven and tossed by the wind."

Pontius Pilate is one who struggled when faced with the decision of what to do with Jesus. When the religious leaders arrested Jesus, and brought Him before Pontius Pilate, the Roman ruler struggled with the decision of what to do with Him. Pilate appealed to Jesus in hopes He would say something that would help Pilate make a decision to free Him. Pilate appeals to the religious leaders without making the decision that his authority would have allowed. He sought out the crowd to make the decision for him by giving them the choice of Barabbas or Jesus. When the soul is not centered, one is never sure what temptations are worth resisting or what sacrifices are worth making.

A soul without Jesus as the center feels constantly vulnerable to people and circumstances. In I Kings 19, Elijah's soul is terrified under the threat of the evil queen Jezebel as he runs and hides from her. Meanwhile, God cares for his soul. God gives his body rest and food, and He speaks to Elijah in His still small voice. He appeals to Elijah to return to the battle. Eventually, Elijah is restored, but only because he found his Center.

A soul without Jesus as the center becomes impatient and discouraged. Numbers 21:4-5 says:

"Then they journeyed from Mount Hor by the Way of the Red Sea, to go around the land of Edom; and the soul of the people became very discouraged on the way. And the people spoke against God and against Moses..."

When the people grew impatient with God's long journey through the wilderness, the literal translation of the text says that *their souls grew short.*

The same usage occurs in Judges 16:16, Samson's soul has no center because he simply rambles from the pursuit of power, to pleasure with women, to revenge. The nagging of one single woman is enough to make this powerful man grow short in soul.

King Saul was a big man with a short soul. When he was to lead Israel against the Philistines, he grew impatient waiting for the prophet Samuel to show up at Gilgal to offer sacrifices. His solution was to take matters into his own hands and offer the sacrifice himself. The result was a broken covenant with God and the destruction of his own soul.

The soul without a center finds its identity in externals. When our souls are not centered in Christ, we are in control of our lives. The opposite of living in faithful dependence on God is lifting our souls up in pride. Habakkuk 2:4 says:

"Behold the proud, His soul is not upright in him; But the just shall live by his faith."

When our soul is not centered in God, we prop ourselves up and define ourselves by our accomplishments, physical appearance, title, or important friends. When we lose any of these things, we lose our identity.

A soul without Jesus at the center is like a house built on sinking sand.

"But everyone who hears these sayings of Mine, and does not do them, will be like a foolish man who built his house on the sand: and the rain descended, the floods came, and the winds blew and beat on that house; and it fell. And great was its fall."
Matthew 7:26-27

On the other hand, the soul has stability when centered on Christ. When we reach out to Him, He lifts us up and we are nurtured and healed. Souls centered in Christ know their Heavenly Father will hold them up through their pain, fear and anxiety. This is the blessed spiritual life, to place our soul each moment in the presence and care of God.

We hold on tightly, often to the wrong things, but if we stay centered on the Lord, His Word and His ways, our testimony can be I Corinthians 15:58:

"We are steadfast, immovable, and always abounding in

the work of the Lord."

Those who have Jesus at the center of their life, find clarity in their personal life which affects their decision making, brings peace of mind and wisdom. Living with Jesus as the center is the abundant life. It impacts everything, but it all begins with you. Once you have experienced this way of life, your family, and everyone you come in contact with will be affected.

God loves family, both biological and spiritual. His desire is to heal, deliver and restore the family to His original blueprint of love, honor and respect. Without applying the principles written in the Word of God to both the natural and spiritual realms of family dynamics we will continue to reap the unhealthy lifestyles and the less than healthy relationships we experience will be perpetuated for generations.

How we live life in the secret place will determine what kind of offspring we produce, biologically and spiritually as well. As it is written in I Corinthians 15:46...however, the spiritual is not first, but the natural, and afterward the spiritual.

This is why it is critical that our lives honor the Lord to the best of our ability and according to the level of understanding in that present moment. We must live out biblical principles (practiced, matured, and perfected) in our own heart before the One who sees it all. We must practice these principles in our closest, most intimate of all relationships with our family in our home. As Philippians 3:12 says:

"Not that I have already attained, or am already perfected; but I press on, that I may lay hold of that for which Christ Jesus has also laid hold of me.

None of us are perfect, but we should be being perfected, working (striving) toward perfection, not as in being perfect, but as in being matured. Colossians 1:28-29 states it best:

Him we preach, warning every man and teaching every man in all wisdom, that we may present every man perfect in Christ Jesus. To this end I also labor, striving according to His working which works in me mightily."

We must come face to face with the reality that Christ is returning for a mature bride.

"...that He might sanctify and cleanse her with the washing of water by the word, that He might present her to Himself a glorious church, not having spot or wrinkle or any such thing, but that she should be holy and without blemish."

Ephesians 5:26-27

Maturity is far more than having knowledge of the Word of God. Knowledge in the mind has to do with IQ or mental intelligence. Knowledge in the heart has to do with EQ, or emotional intelligence and maturity, and knowledge in the spirit, I refer to as SQ, or spiritual intelligence and maturity.

A Christian can know the Word in their spirit because the Word is spirit, but not allow the Spirit of the Word to renew their mind to heal and mature their emotions.

If you want to have some fun, I suggest you take the personality test found in the book "The Color Code" by Taylor Hartman. It has helped me to better understand myself, my family members, and the diversity in church staff personalities. I have learned how they play off each other's weaknesses, and despise and compete with each other's strengths. Every personality is both weak in some ways and strong in others.

It is so funny to watch couples be attracted and think they are perfect for each other...until marriage and the real you pops out. Surprise! I laughed out loud when one young man said it this way, "Three days after marriage, I woke up one morning and said to God, 'I think I married the bride of Satan; what happened to the woman I knew before I married her?'"

Married couples who are making marriage work will tell you that it only works if you work it. The same principles for marriage apply to all relationships, especially those in the life of His church body found in Ephesians 5:31-32:

"For this reason a man shall leave his father and mother and be joined to his wife, and the two shall become one flesh." This is a great mystery, but I speak concerning Christ and the church."

The mystery of how relationships work is not one that is completely hidden from us. This great mystery can be found and worked out in the wisdom of the Word of God.

"For this commandment which I command you today is not too mysterious for you, nor is it far off. It is not in heaven, that you should say, 'Who will ascend into heaven for us and bring it to us, that we may hear it and do it?' Nor is it beyond the sea, that you should say, 'Who will go over the sea for us and bring it to us, that we may hear it and do it?' But the word is very near you, in your mouth and in your heart, that you may do it."See, I have set before you today life and good, death and evil, in that I command you today to

love the LORD your God, to walk in His ways, and to keep His commandments, His statutes, and His judgments, that you may live and multiply; and the LORD your God will bless you in the land which you go to possess. But if your heart turns away so that you do not hear and are drawn away, and worship other gods and serve them, I announce to you today that you shall surely perish; you shall not prolong your days in the land which you cross over the Jordan to go in and possess. I call heaven and earth as witnesses today against you, that I have set before you life and death, blessing and cursing; therefore choose life, that both you and your descendants may live; that you may love the LORD your God, that you may obey His voice, and that you may cling to Him, for He is your life and the length of your days; and that you may dwell in the land which the LORD swore to give to your fathers, to Abraham, Isaac, and Jacob, to give them."

Deuteronomy 30:11-20

For any relationship to work, whether it is God and man, husband and wife, parent and child, at work, school or with a neighbor, there must be two willing parties who are willing to work it out. Sometimes it may feel more like they are emotionally duking it out.

"Therefore, my beloved, as you have always obeyed, not as in my presence only, but now much more in my absence, work out your own salvation with fear and trembling."

Philippians 2:12

I have a saying, "I am not going to lose my salvation over this." Or when speaking with a close relationship I would express it like this, "I am not going to get my britches in a knot." Either phrase simply means, I am going to work it out in my own emotions, come to a place of peace between me and God, and leave the circumstance or the person that I can't change in God's hands. These phrases are another way of stating the expression we are most familiar with, "Let go and let God."

Applying the truth of God's Word is a process of working out the wrong, and working in the right. The process reminds me of the saying in Alcoholics Anonymous, "Keep coming back, it works if you work it." And "You can't think your way into a new way of living... you have to live your way into a new way of thinking." This idea applies in every area: attitude, relationships, finances, priorities, core values and life principles.

The bottom line is our emotional maturity level will be evident in the choices and responses we have every day, in every dimension of life. There is no way of getting away from or getting around the truth. We live out the reality (as living proof) of who we really are and how much of God's love we really have experienced; it shows up (or off) in everyday life. The purity of our motives, passion in our heart, and compassion for others is determined by the quality of our intellectual, emotional and spiritual health.

This fact is clearly demonstrated in American youth culture. The Ten Commandments, prayer and God consciousness have been under siege and attacked by secular humanism in the hopes of being removed from the very fiber of our nation. It all begins with breaking down and reforming the ideology of young people in our schools. Teachers have the power to shape our nation. The Good Teacher, Jesus, through the power of the Holy Spirit, has been sent to teach us the way that leads to life, but we have rejected Him and chosen our own way and our young have lost their way.

"Now behold, one came and said to Him, 'Good

Teacher, what good thing shall I do that I may have eternal life?' So He said to him, 'Why do you call Me good? No one is good but One, that is, God...'"
Matthew 19:16-17

Educators are perpetrating secular humanism, which is the worship of self. This philosophy is the New Age religion of the United States, and it has permeated the doctrine of the church. There is a hatred of truth, and a new interpretation of truth according to man's wisdom.

"Blessed are those who do His commandments, that they may have the right to the tree of life, and may enter through the gates into the city. But outside are dogs and sorcerers and sexually immoral and murderers and idolaters, and whoever loves and practices a lie. I, Jesus, have sent My angel to testify to you these things in the churches. I am the Root and the Offspring of David, the Bright and Morning Star."
Revelations 22:14-15

"So God created man in His own image; in the image of God He created him; male and female He created them..."
Genesis 1:27

"And He answered and said to them, 'Have you not read that He who made them at the beginning 'made them male and female,'"
Matthew 19:4

"Therefore God also gave them up to uncleanness, in the lusts of their hearts, to dishonor their bodies among themselves, who exchanged the truth of God for the lie, and worshiped and served the creature rather than the Creator, who is blessed forever. Amen. For this reason God gave them up to vile passions.

For even their women exchanged the natural use for what is against nature."

Romans1:24-26

Prayer has been removed from the American schools and the gates of hell have been opened to our children. Our young are not eating from the tree of life. They are eating from the tree of the knowledge of good and evil, and are exposed and vulnerable to every kind of evil.

"Train up a child in the way he should go, And when he is old he will not depart from it."

Proverbs 22:6

The truth, whether it is used for good or evil, depends on interpretation of the one who is teaching. This world system teaches self-gratification is the way to happiness. Give me what I want, and I will be happy. If I am not happy it's your fault. Therefore, I must remove myself from you, I will cut you, demoralize you, hurt you, get rid of you and then I will be happy.

We will be talking more about Healing Waters weekend in Chapter Three, but I can tell you, when people come through the Healing Waters weekend, we help them navigate the troubled waters in their soul. The pain we suffer in life is related to our own sin, or others' sinful behaviors done against us. Jesus understands our suffering, although He didn't suffer because He sinned, He suffered because of our sin. As it says in, Philippians 2:5-8:

"Let this mind be in you which was also in Christ Jesus, who, being in the form of God, did not consider it robbery to be equal with God, but made Himself of no reputation, taking the form of a bondservant, and coming in the likeness of men. And being found

in appearance as a man, He humbled Himself and became obedient to the point of death, even the death of the cross."

Jesus, the very image of God, humbled Himself and became obedient. It is the goal of the devil to steal, kill and destroy. His strategy is to tempt man to pride himself in being his own god and then use the very ones God created in His image to destroy, mar, disfigure and maim His image in others.

Many Christians can quote multitudes of Scripture verses and claim to have great wisdom but their lives are in shambles and their relationships are in distress. Their life skills are infantile, their relational and communication skills underdeveloped and their ability to process the challenges of life lacks wisdom and discretion. They have no biblical core values that guide their life choices. The Bible gives us the keys to grow up spiritually, mentally and emotionally in Ephesians 5:15 AMP as it says:

"...speaking the truth in love, [you] may grow up in all things into Him who is the head-Christ."

None of us in and of ourselves have absolute truth. We all have a measure of truth or a part of truth, as Scripture reveals in I Corinthians 13:11-12:

"When I was a child, I spoke as a child, I understood as a child, I thought as a child; but when I became a man, I put away childish things. For now we see in a mirror, dimly, but then face to face. Now I know in part, but then I shall know just as I also am known."

Often our method and means of communicating hinders others ability to receive from us. We tend to mix our measure of truth with our opinion of the truth, wrapped up in our personality's delivery of a part of truth which in turn causes resistance to the measure of truth. The hearer then justifies dismissing the measure of truth that God is endeavoring to reveal because it comes through as a broken vessel just like us. The result is no one ends up hearing Him.

A great example of this phenomenon is found in two personality types referred to as Red and a White by Taylor Hartman in his book "The Color Code". Red personalities care deeply about people, but are more interested in being right than being sensitive to others' feelings. A White personality can be very self-focused and interpret everything based on their emotions.

A hypothetical conversation between the two personalities would be similar to this: Red says with enthusiasm and passion, "Everybody knows that, what is wrong with you?!" A typical White responds with timid feelings and apologies, "I am so sorry. I don't know what is wrong with me, it seems everybody says there is something wrong, please just tell me what I should do."

Whites have a tendency to set themselves up to be the victims of a Red's tendency to be king of the hill, when in actuality, the way relationships are intended to work is the strength of the Red personality builds up the weaknesses of the White, and the White helps the Red be more relational.

"So one man sharpens [and influences] another [through discussion]."
$\qquad$ Proverbs 27:17 AMP

"The voice of one crying in the wilderness: "Prepare the way of the LORD; Make straight in the desert A highway for our God. Every valley shall be exalted

And every mountain and hill brought low; The crooked places shall be made straight And the rough places smooth; The glory of the LORD shall be revealed, And all flesh shall see it together; For the mouth of the LORD has spoken."

Isaiah 40:3-5

The Lord desires to make our crooked places (twisted mindsets) straight, our valleys (weaknesses) raised up, our mountains (pride) brought low, (humbled) and the rough (edgy) places in our personality made smooth (pleasant). To do these things, The Lord uses our closest relationships. He uses them to confront us in our methods. Sometimes we shoot His messenger with the attitude, "Who do you think you are," 'Mr. Right?' When was the last time you took a good look in the mirror at yourself?"

Sometimes we need to be reminded that God can use a donkey to intervene in our lives and speak a word to us, just like he did with Balaam in Numbers 22:27-30:

"And when the donkey saw the Angel of the LORD, she lay down under Balaam; so Balaam's anger was aroused, and he struck the donkey with his staff. Then the LORD opened the mouth of the donkey, and she said to Balaam, 'What have I done to you, that you have struck me these three times' And Balaam said to the donkey, 'Because you have abused me. I wish there were a sword in my hand, for now I would kill you!' So the donkey said to Balaam, 'Am I not your donkey on which you have ridden, ever since I became yours, to this day? Was I ever disposed to do this to you?' And he said, 'No.'"

Many times someone will say to me, "Pastor I want you to tell me the truth, where do you see weakness in my leadership skills, and where do you see I need to grow?" I have found these kinds of conversations are an opportunity to test my personality weaknesses and my leadership strength, not those of the individual asking the question. It is usually after these heart-to-heart conversations, speaking the truth (my partial truth) in love, that there is often some kind of melt down in the relationship.

More times than not, those conversations silently blow up, and the once dedicated, faithful person, who would take the proverbial bullet for you, slips out the back door. These conversations can also lead to blow ups when you touch their stuff. They make sure everyone knows what a prideful, arrogant leader you are and they feel they need to save everyone else from being abused by you.

It is at these times I often need reminding that the donkey was beaten just for looking out for Balaam's best interest.

> *"Then the LORD opened Balaam's eyes, and he saw the Angel of the LORD standing in the way with His drawn sword in His hand; and he bowed his head and fell flat on his face. And the Angel of the LORD said to him, "Why have you struck your donkey these three times? Behold, I have come out to stand against you, because your way is perverse before Me. The donkey saw Me and turned aside from Me these three times. If she had not turned aside from Me, surely I would also have killed you by now, and let her live."*
> Numbers 22: 31-33

Oh the joys of pastoring, I love a picture that I found on Facebook. It's from a scene in the "Pirates Of The Caribbean™" where Jack Sparrow is running from the mob that is chasing him. The caption reads, "Be a Pastor they said, It'll be fun they said." Every time I see it, I LOL!

Often when God is using someone to intervene in our lives, His intended purpose is to save us from ourselves. We see it as an interference and intrusion into our little world of ways and means, instead of an intervention with His intention to bring healing and health. We need to be reminded the cross is both horizontal and vertical.

The first five of the Ten Commandments are vertical, and are about our relationship with God. The last five are horizontal, and are about our relationship with mankind. How we see ourselves through the cross is directly related and connected to how we view others. When our identity is fractured and fragile, we are not able to receive correction, instruction and discipline.

One of the books God used in my life to teach important biblical core values to live by was "Seven Habits of Highly Effective People" by Stephen Covey. I learned of the book while attending Skill Path workshops which helped me immensely in learning to navigate the challenge of conflict resolution, anger management, and dealing with difficult personalities.

We all know that Jesus came to save, heal, and deliver, which is the whole Gospel. We need to be coached on how to practically live out the Good News, not just in our head, but in everyday life. The Evangelical Church does okay with sharing the salvation message. Most Christians believe and can quote John 3:6-8 which says:

"That which is born of the flesh is flesh, and that which is born of the Spirit is spirit. Do not marvel that I said to you, 'You must be born again.' The wind blows where it wishes, and you hear the sound of it, but cannot tell where it comes from and where it goes. So is everyone who is born of the Spirit."

And Luke 19: 9-10:

"...and Jesus said to him, 'Today salvation has come to this house, because he also is a son of Abraham; for the Son of Man has come to seek and to save that which was lost.'"

The Charismatic Church does okay with sharing the healing message and praying for healing.

"But He was wounded for our transgressions, He was bruised for our iniquities; The chastisement for our peace was upon Him, And by His stripes we are healed."

Isaiah 53:5

"...who Himself bore our sins in His own body on the tree, that we, having died to sins, might live for righteousness—by whose stripes you were healed."

1 Peter 2:24

However, most of the church world doesn't want to touch or even learn about the deliverance part of the Gospel message. There is fear of the realm of deliverance as if it is something separate from salvation and healing.

"The Spirit of the LORD is upon Me, Because He has anointed Me To preach the gospel to the poor; He has sent Me to heal the brokenhearted, To proclaim liberty to the captives And recovery of sight to the blind, To set at liberty those who are oppressed; 19 To proclaim the acceptable year of the LORD."

Luke 4:18-19

"Little children, let no one deceive you. He who prac-

39

tices righteousness is righteous, just as He is righteous. He who sins is of the devil, for the devil has sinned from the beginning. For this purpose the Son of God was manifested, that He might destroy the works of the devil."

1 John 3:7-8

"...who delivered us from so great a death, and does deliver us; in whom we trust that He will still deliver us..."

2 Corinthians 1:10

Deliverance for the believer is freedom from the strongholds that hinder, afflict, torment, oppress, suppress and depress the human soul through the blood and name of Jesus Christ. It is sad to see so many professing Christ who have been redeemed by His blood, but are living so far below the life of freedom that He died to give us. There is a deficit in the heart of believers of truly knowing that we are fearfully and wonderfully made. Instead many Christians are living fearful and wonder why they were even born.

The healing path the Lord brings each individual through is different for everyone. For some people there is an encounter like the Star Wars movies with an exciting dramatic evil versus good confrontation and, a 'tah dah' victory that makes everything different. I used to be jealous of those who had a testimony like that, wishing that was my experience. My testimony is more like what is written in Job 23:8-13:

"Look, I go forward, but He is not there, And backward, but I cannot perceive Him; When He works on the left hand, I cannot behold Him; When He turns to the right hand, I cannot see Him. But He knows the way that I take; When He has tested me, I shall come forth as gold. My foot has held fast to His steps;

40

I have kept His way and not turned aside. I have not departed from the commandment of His lips; I have treasured the words of His mouth More than my necessary food. But He is unique, and who can make Him change? And whatever His soul desires, that He does."

My journey has been a quiet, gentle, no fanfare one; just consistent, forward, advancement through obedience and patient endurance. He has done marvelous things and brought obvious victory that has been made evident over time much like the following testimony of Denise Donegan:

"I have had a personal appointment with Care Ministers, and attended Healing Waters weekend. My journey of healing has been different than others. It has been good, although I didn't experience freedom in the same way as others testify. I wanted so much to be able to jump and shout, 'Yippee! I am totally FREE!' But for me, I have found the Healing Waters materials that were given me are like gold that I search out. From it, I have learned that a critical part of healing and deliverance is repenting and taking back your authority.

I like to personalize Ephesians 6:10-18 in the Passion Translation:

'Now finally, my beloved (Denise), be supernaturally infused with strength through your life-union with the Lord Jesus Christ. Stand strong with the force of His explosive power flowing in and through you. Put on the full suit of armor that God wears when He goes into battle, so that you will be protected as you take a stand against the evil strategies of the Accuser! Your hand to hand combat is not with human beings, but with the highest principalities and authorities oper-

ating in rebellion under the heavenly realms; for they are a powerful class of demon gods and evil spirits that hold this dark world in bondage. Because of this, you must wear all the armor that God provides so you're protected (Denise) as you confront the Slanderer, for you (Denise) are destined for all things and will rise victorious!'

Before receiving ministry, I believed a lot of half-truths. For example, I would have a negative thought, and then it would become a string of negative thoughts. They were partly my own thoughts, but I got the sense there was a tormenting spirit fueling them. I would repent of everything I could think of: jealousy, resentment, judgement, self-pity and self-hatred to try to get relief, which I would find for a short time, but then would be back on the never ending wheel of tears and frustration.

After receiving deliverance ministry, the gift of discernment and wisdom brought to light what I was fighting against. It was spiritual and not the people I love. I used the teaching and tools I received to walk step by step into a purpose- fulfilled life. I have been given helpful materials and teaching such as; "The Heart of an Orphan vs the Heart of Sonship," "I am who I AM says I am," which is all Scriptures. These and other materials have all played such an important role in my life to walk out my salvation with fear and trembling.

After Healing Waters, I attended the Care Minister training and have since joined the monthly Care Ministry team training. I feel so honored and blessed to now be a part of the *He Cares for Me* ministry team. I have learned through this whole process how to take back my authority. I have learned who I am, and most importantly how my Father sees me! The Lord has given me a vision that He is my Father God who is big and strong. In the vision, I saw myself standing behind Him with His right arm held like a stop sign. He is my protector and the lover of my soul!"

The members of the Care Ministry team know it's not us, or the ministry of *He Cares for Me*, or an event on the calendar that changes one's life. Those things are simply means that God uses to bring about His desired end. I encourage you to read all of Psalm 18 for a more complete picture of the God who delivers, especially the verses that resound the testimony of many who have come through Healing Waters, expressed in verses 1-3, 16-19 and 25.

Intercession
A Defining Moment

I have been serving the Lord since I received the gift of salvation in January 1977. Whatever my hand found to do, I did it with all my strength, all my heart and to the best of my ability. From the very beginning of my walk with Him, I have jumped into whatever the Lord put on my heart to do. I have always believed it is simple, although many times I made it complicated. He said His yoke is easy and His burden is light, but I often made it heavy. I am so glad He loves me and bears with me in spite of me because His love does bear all things.

Over a 30 year period of time, God has led me to different streams in the body of Christ for cleansing, healing and refreshing. There were different healing ministries that would occasionally hold a healing conference in different cities throughout New England. All were wonderful and were used to bring a measure of freedom to my soul.

I am very grateful for what I received, although I never came away with a sense of being equipped with spiritual authority, clarity of how to bring others through to healing or confidence to do so. That is not to say that those ministries were the reason why, those were just the feelings I had. Evangelical churches may offer their members counseling appointments and Charismatic churches may offer prayer at the altar on a Sunday morning, but where does one go to receive healing for soul wounds? Deliverance is often the ministry in the church that is ignored or neglected.

God used a defining moment for me in my personal life. As a lead pastor, in my own church, I was not training leaders to minister deliverance or offering deliverance ministry, but that was about to change forever! One of my family members had a spiritual, emotional, mental, financial, relational crisis in their life. I couldn't offer to care for their need, or find a place locally to send them for crisis intervention. I diligently searched, finding only one that had trained ministers who offered deliverance and healing.

To receive ministry it required flying to the middle of the country, renting a car, booking a hotel, and paying out of pocket $1,200.00 for 12 hours of ministry over a 4 day period, which insurance didn't cover. I was in shock and thought, "WOW! Really God? Is healing only for those who can afford to pay that kind of price?"

My heart was overwhelmed with sorrow, mixed with anger, frustration and feelings of hopelessness. I cried out to God, "Why? Why was there nowhere for them to go for help?" All the years I had served counseling others, and now one of my own family members needed help, and I couldn't help them. I knew I was too close to the situation for them to be comfortable with me, and I wasn't sure of how or what to do even if they were willing for me to help them.

I love how God uses everything the devil means for evil and turns it around for good! The Lord uses what happens in our personal lives to set us up for breakthrough and birth something beautiful.

As I wept in travail and interceded for my loved one,

God spoke to me, "Do for others what I have done for you."

I responded, "But Lord it's taken years for me to struggle through to healing. There has to be a better way than the 40 year wilderness journey to the promised land of healing."

I wasn't sure what I was to do, so after seeking the Lord for quite some time, I just started typing what was in my heart on my laptop for days, which turned into weeks and months.

Over the next year, two confirmations came. God used a man named Merrick Finn. I knew Merrick from Community Christian Fellowship in Lowell, Massachusetts. Merrick called to ask if he and his wife, Mary, could meet with me. He felt God was calling him into a deeper level of ministering to the wounded soul. Every time he prayed, he felt the Lord impressed him to call me. I met with them several times as God was unfolding His plan for Merrick to be a key part of *He Cares for Me.* Following is Merrick's testimony:

> When I reached out to Pastor Marlene several years ago, it became clear that we shared the same dream of wanting to help individuals experience the promise in His Word of being free indeed, and to walk in the Spirit.
>
> *"If you abide in my word, you are My disciples indeed. And you shall know the truth and the truth shall make you free."*
>
> John 8:31-32

The core issue we agreed on was that some of the more popular tools being used in the Body of Christ ostensibly for this purpose, that we had both trained in, did not fit with our gut feeling and understanding of how God wanted to equip us to pursue the dream.

As my own healing journey was evolving, I was keenly aware of how much more inner freedom my soul longed for. Around this time the Lord was gracious to show me the beauty and simplicity of working through a simple prayer ministry model/approach introduced to me through my home church.

I personally experienced a greater freedom in my soul, and recognized how this kind of personal approach using facilitated conversation based on touch, pain points, waiting on the Spirit to reveal the root issue, and praying for the Lord to bring clarity and resolution is so very powerfully liberating.

During this period, I was experiencing a greater level of the Father's love through several different ministries. In early 2000, I had received a powerful revelation, and in 2005 a significant impartation of the Father's love as He began to draw me deeper still. He revealed I had been carrying an orphan heart all my life. We all have been wounded and in some measure have an orphan heart.

It became evident that I had been talking about walking in the Spirit, but walking mostly in the flesh with a religious mind-set striving to please God. The revelation that Father loves me just as much as He loves His Son Jesus began to unlock the depths of the cry of my heart to my God. Knowing that Jesus came to redeem my spirit and my soul from the torment of Satan and hell is one thing, but to really apprehend the deeper place of His fullness, I needed to know the Father's heart intimately for myself.

In short, as I was pursuing more prayer ministry, the Lord revealed that I was double-minded in my soul. While I had no clue about this, I knew I felt stuck, but had no idea how to move forward. Once this issue was identified and resolved in my heart and soul, walking in true sonship became possible. The Father healed me from living with an orphan heart orientation, and unlocked my heart to know His rest and genuine peace.

In July 2015 my wife and I were invited to join Pastor Marlene as she launched the HCFM ministry. As a Board member and Assistant Director, I have been a part of the ministry development, teaching and training Care Ministers and teaching on the Father's love at the Healing Waters weekend.

Truly, my greatest joy is seeing His sons and daughters coming to know His love, meeting them right where they are on their journey to wholeness and becoming free indeed. It is a joy to fellowship, worship, pray and grow together with the Care Team!

These things I have spoken to you, that My joy may remain in you, and that your joy may be full.
John 15:11

God keeps His promises!

Another confirmation came from Martha Temple. I had known Martha for over twenty years. She and I had been youth ministers at different churches back in the day. Her son and my daughter were in the same school together, and became friends, and many years later, married. Now after all these years, God gave Martha several dreams about working with me, knowing it had to do with deliverance ministry.

I spent many months with Merrick and Martha praying and preparing before we launched the ministry. Merrick and Martha are my very dear friends, and my life has been enriched by them as they serve with me in *He Cares for Me*. I am so grateful the Lord chose and called us for such a time as this. Together we earnestly seek Him for wisdom and diligently guard what He has done in our hearts and ministry.

"I have called you friends, for all things that I heard from My Father I have made known to you. You did not choose Me, but I chose you and appointed you that you should go and bear fruit, and that your fruit should remain, that whatever you ask the Father in My name He may give you. These things I command you, that you love one another."

John 15:15-17

As time passed, I continued typing what is now the model and manual for the ministry. What evolved, out of prayer and simple obedience to put in writing, was the teaching for Healing Waters teacher and participants guides, Care Minister training, guidelines for Personal and Marriage retreats, two hour ministry appointments and group retreats we host at Kingston Cottage, as well as applications and disclaimer documents. Wow! I could see the plan of God unfolding. He was birthing a ministry of deliverance and healing. Little did we know, it would have such a powerful impact for so many lives on every level.

There are 14 critical steps needed to experience lasting freedom. Unless these steps are applied one is not going to be able to secure lasting freedom and declare:

"Whom the Son sets free is free indeed."

Deliverance is not something we can do apart from His mercy and grace because it is *"'...not by our might nor by our power, but by My Spirit,' says the Lord."* Zachariah 4:6

Deliverance is not a one-time thing, it is a lifestyle of learning to walk in His holiness.

Following is a list of the steps that must be applied if one is to experience lasting fruit that remains. This is the Holy Spirit kind of fruit that becomes evident in your everyday life. This is the fruit that Galatians 5:22-23 lists, which is love, joy, peace, longsuffering, kindness, goodness, faithfulness, gentleness and self-control. It's that fruit that then qualifies us to minister to others out of a place of our own freedom.

1. *Humility: humble ourselves*
2. *Submit: to the Lord and His Word*
3. *Acknowledge: we have sinned*
4. *Confess: our sin and that we need to be saved from it*
5. *Repent: for our sinful actions, offenses, disobedience and omissions*
6. *Renounce: evil wicked deeds and thoughts*
7. *Release: bitter root judgments*
8. *Break: covenants, curses, inner vows and soul ties*
9. *Discharge and dismiss: principalities and powers*
10. *Expose and dismantle: lies of the enemy*
11. *Reclaim: kingdom authority that we surrendered through sin*
12. *Declare and decree: the finished work of the cross and the promises of God*
13. *Be filled: with the power of the Spirit, walking in the love, joy and peace of Christ*
14. *Be diligent: to continue to fight the good fight, ruling over sin, reigning with Him*

Prior to the ministry development of *He Cares for Me*, I found in most counseling sessions that the counselee was focused on what was done against them by others. They needed to forgive and receive forgiveness for the sin they had done against others, but there is so much more that needs to be addressed with care and prayer.

Inception
Of A Ministry

Many years ago at a Generation Conference in Utica, New York, Jude Fouquier, Pastor of The City Church, prophesied that I would have a ministry of healing and deliverance. Now all these many years later, God has used me to birth *He Cares for Me*, a non-profit ministry of healing and deliverance that has three components:

1) Healing Waters (HW) -In the spring and fall we offer a healing weekend for believers who attend a local church, have a pastoral referral and are committed to their healing journey. There are twelve Care Ministers that serve every healing weekend, and we only accept twelve applications to ensure every person registered receives quality care. Sessions are held Friday 6-10pm, and Saturday 10 am-6pm. There are ten teaching sessions, followed by personal ministry after each. Categories cover everything from the womb to the tomb, or in other words, from life to death. Each session includes teaching on the following topics:

1. Laying the foundation from the Word for deliverance and healing

2. Holy Spirit identifying open doors

3. Addictions: drugs, alcohol, pornography, media, food, hoarding, shopping, ministry, etc.

4. Loss and grief: divorce, miscarriage, trauma, disasters, loss of a loved one, emotional death of a

He Cares For Me

relationship, death of a vision

5. Relationships: self/others, idolatry and distorted self-centeredness, co-dependency

6. Breaking covenants: curses, occult practices, horoscope, fortune telling, hypnosis, Free Masonry, religious spirits, false religions, Wiccan, New Age, angel cards and idolatry

7. Abuse: emotional, sexual, mental, physical, self-hatred, self-abuse, self-mutilation, self-gratification, fornication, same sex attraction and gender confusion

8. Illness: mental, emotional, physical and spiritual-post-traumatic stress, medication, depression, suicide, eating disorders and cutting. Sickness and disease have 5 components: natural, physical, mental, emotional and spiritual.

9. Natural and Spiritual authority: submission and obedience, covering and blessing.

10. Principles to maintain freedom: humility, confession, repentance, renounce, forgive, renewing covenant, restoration, rejoice, return to give thanks, walking in spiritual authority and remaining free.

After the first teaching session, Laying a foundation from the Word for deliverance and healing, the Care Ministry team washes the feet of the registrants, anoints them with oil and prays over them, asking for the anointing of the Holy Spirit to break every yoke and open the prison doors for the oppressed to go free.

The following is a testimony from Louisa who attended Healing Waters weekend:

"The first teaching session was concluded with a foot washing. The presence of God was so real to me as my feet were washed with the fragrant essential oil water I started to weep uncontrollably. I felt so safe and cared for as I melted in God's peace. I knew He was preparing my heart to open and to receive all He had for me that weekend. Within days after receiving ministry, I had an opportunity to exercise my new freedom in Christ only to find, it was real, really real!!!

I was walking in a new level of authority to rule over my own soul and the emotionally toxic person I was dealing with didn't have the usual effect on me. I found myself not reacting with panic and fear but I was now responding in wisdom and peace which disarmed the situation. My experience with Healing Waters weekend was life changing."

During the sixth session, Breaking covenants, we believe after repentance and breaking covenants with the occult and powers of darkness, it is important to take communion together and declare the power of the blood of Jesus.

During the last session, Principles to maintain freedom, we celebrate. Those who attended the weekend testify of their freedom, and we worship and rejoice. We end by laying hands and anointing them with frankincense oil to send them forward to serve the Lord in the power and freedom of His Spirit.

We use the 23rd Psalm as a model for healing, and we break it down like this:

"The LORD is my shepherd":
Starting with confession- Jesus Christ is the Lord, Savior and Master Shepherd of my life. I choose to trust God the Father, God the Son and God the Holy Spirit.
"I shall not want":

I surrender and submit the wants and desires of my heart, He gives me the desires of His heart, and He wants His best for me!

"He makes me to lie down in green pastures":
I choose to lie down and rest so I can receive from Him: only then will He reproduce Himself in me.

"He leads me beside the still waters":
I am willing to let Him lead me to be still beside the healing waters.

"He restores my soul":
He alone makes me whole, renews my mind, regenerates my heart, rebuilds the old waste places and restores the years that the locusts have eaten.

"He leads me in the paths of righteousness for His name's sake":
His ways are righteous and by His grace and my choice to submit, He keeps me on the right path.

"Yea, though I walk through the valley of the shadow of death":
I will make the descent and walk through the valley of the shadow of death.

"I will fear no evil; for You are with me":
His perfect love casts out my fear, because love and fear cannot co-exist. Fear has two meanings: forget everything and run, or face everything and rise. The choice is mine.

"Your rod and Your staff, they comfort me":
I accept His disciplines with the rod of correction as He draws me near with His staff to comfort me.

"You prepare a table before me in the presence of

my enemies":
He doesn't always deliver me out of situations. He often delivers me in the midst of them. I learn to rule with Him in the midst of my enemies. He displays His power by parading me in front of my enemy to display His victory in me.

"You anoint my head with oil; My cup runs over."
He is the Balm of Gilead, the anointing that breaks the yoke of bondage. He anoints me with the oil of gladness. His oil of healing runs over my head, runs into my heart and runs out of my mouth and life. Freely I have received and freely I give.

"Surely goodness and mercy shall follow me all the days of my life":
His thoughts toward me are for good and not for evil. I have a future and a hope. I abide under the shadow of the Almighty, and I cleave to the vine who is Christ. I am blessed and highly favored. Bad things may happen but God is good all the time.

"And I will dwell in the house of the LORD forever":
Here on this earth my (body) temple is the dwelling place of the Lord. He is magnified corporately (His church) in the house of the Lord. He has made me a home in heaven with Him forever.

2) Twice a year following a Healing Waters weekend, we offer Care Minister Training (CMT) on a Saturday from 10am- 6pm. Training involves biblical teaching with hands on experience with deliverance. Those being trained have attended a Healing Waters weekend, been referred by their pastor, and sense a call from God to be trained to minister healing and deliverance to others.

They choose to live a life in pursuit of the Holy One, with continued freedom in their own life. Deliverance ministry is not something we try out. It is a calling to a lifestyle of purity, freedom, accountability and discipleship. Those who choose to be trained, practice openness and honesty with others on the Care Team in obedience to James 5:16:

"Confess your trespasses to one another, and pray for one another, that you may be healed. The effective, fervent prayer of a righteous man avails much."

The Vision of *He Cares for Me*:

- To see the body of Christ rise up as the End Time army of the Lord referring to Ezekiel's vision of the dry bones.

- Equip Care Ministers that are clothed in His righteousness with the anointing of the Holy Spirit to minister in the power of His love.

- To see believers filled with the Zoe (life) of God, releasing the spirit of prophecy, decreeing and declaring the Word of the Lord with power and authority.

- Men and women under authority, in unity, and walking in peace, fully equipped and ready to minister.

- Care Ministers armed with the Word of God to displace lies with truth, thus renewing the mind, and applying the healing balm of Gilead to broken hearts.

- To prepare church lay leaders to minister to those in their congregation now and the multitudes to come when He pours out His Spirit in these last days.

The Mission:

- To teach and train leaders referred by their

pastor to serve in the ministry of *He Cares for Me* "Healing Waters" weekend, and to serve their local church in the ministry of healing the soul.

- Teach believers to walk in the authority of the Name and blood of Christ that gives them power over the works of darkness.

- To equip them with tools that disarm strongholds that keep them in the prison house of their own soul through iniquitous, innocent, ignorant, imputed or intentional sin.

At the end of each teaching session, there is a time of worship and personal prayer ministry, laying on of hands, and anointing with oil for healing. Participants finish the weekend by offering their lives as a living sacrifice set apart by God for holy service, ready and equipped to minister freedom to those sent by God, who are approved by their pastor for personal ministry. For applications, disclaimer and more information, see our website:

www.HeCaresForMe.org

He Cares For Me will serve to strengthen local churches offering ministry of healing and deliverance in the following ways:

A. Train local church leaders to serve and support what is presently being offered in their local church.

B. Equip Care Ministers for the Luke 4:18 mission to heal the brokenhearted and bring freedom to the captives. We encourage local church pastors to refer their congregants to attend the "Healing Waters" weekend as a part of their journey of healing and equipping all believers with the tools to walk in freedom.

A Care Minister is a prayer coach, not a counselor. The coach's job is to lead people to a place of truth for themselves. Then the person they are coaching is responsible before God for what they do with the truth, whereas a prayer counselor may tell others what the Bible says, and tell them what they should do about it.

The Care Minister

Helps the person to identify their need:

1. What is the Holy Spirit revealing to you?

2. What is He showing you, or speaking to you?

3. What do you sense in your heart?

4. What is it you want the Lord to do for you?

Doesn't assume, but asks questions:

1. Have you acknowledged and received Jesus Christ as your Savior?

2. Have you confessed your sins and received forgiveness, and have you forgiven others?

3. Is He the Lord of your life, have have you given Him priority and authority in every area of your life?

4. Do you trust that His ways are right and true, and that He has your best interest at heart?

Leads participants to the Word of God:

1. What does the Word say about trusting Him? (He knows all about your situation).

2. Do you believe He is able to make all things beautiful in His time?

3. Are you willing to surrender your will to His will and invite Him into the situation?

4. What does the Bible say about Him providing for your need?

Keeps participants directed and focused:

1. Don't allow participants to carry on and on with gory details about the situation.

2. Don't allow participants to control the time of prayer (by being overly talkative).

3. Establish that the church altar is not the place for a counseling appointment.

4. Encourage participants to connect with a leader for additional care ministry and discipleship.

5. Suggest a personal ministry appointment if needed.

Encourages participants to make a decision to obey what they know to be truth:

1. They will give an account before the Lord with what they did with truth.

2. Have them pray out loud to confess, repent, renounce, re-establish and return to a place of trust and confession of faith.

Coaches participants to exercise their own authority using the:

1. Sword of the Spirit: I cut myself free from "_____."

2. Belt of truth: I walk in truth and the truth keeps me from the evil one.

3. Shield of faith: I quench the fiery dart of the lies.

4. Helmet of salvation: my mind is covered in the blood of the risen Christ.

5. Breastplate of righteousness: I am protected by His righteousness.

6. Shoes of the gospel of peace: I crush Satan under my feet when I walk in peace and trample on

the lies of the enemy.

7. Decree and declare their position as a child of God. I am seated in heavenly place with Christ.

Prays a prayer of agreement and blessing:

1. Agreeing with them in faith, along with them, not doing it for them.

2. Laying on of hands, anointing with oil the front of the head (conscious mind) and back of the head (reticular, subconscious mind) where memories are stored.

Care Ministers train through role-play coaching prayer sessions and they develop their coaching skills by ministering to one another at the (CMT) monthly meetings. They practice coaching prayer with both lion-like and lamb-like methods.

1. Lion-like: firm but loving authority with a person who is all over the place emotionally and mentally.

2. Lamb-like: gentle, but assertive authority with a person who is hesitant and fearful to speak up.

The Care Ministry Team members are not medical, psychiatric care providers or licensed counselors. They are volunteers made up of licensed ministers and leaders who have been referred by their local pastor. They are trained and equipped to offer prayer, in addition to biblical principles, which if applied to one's personal life, have the potential for healing. The Lord desires His Church to be healed and equipped to minister healing and freedom to others.

We believe and practice the anointing of oil and the laying on of hands, for the healing of body, soul and spirit as found in James 5:14-15:

"Is anyone among you sick? Let him call for the elders of the church, and let them pray over him, anointing him with oil in the name of the Lord. And the prayer of faith will save the sick, and the Lord will raise him up. And if he has committed sins, he will be forgiven."

As Christians, we don't have to carry the pain, disappointment, and anger of yesterday into our todays and allow them multiply in our tomorrows. That's Good News!

When believers walk in the truth of His Word, we have the joy of receiving forgiveness every day and new mercies every morning! Every sunset closes the end of one day, and every sunrise is God's assurance we have another day to do, to be, to have, to love and to live better.

Before I knew the Lord, I lived misguided and misinformed, and I misunderstood the realities of life. I dabbled in the occult, went to fortune tellers, read horoscopes, and even worked a short time for a fortune teller. As the Scripture says in Jonah, I didn't know right from wrong and couldn't discern my left from my right hand.

"And should I not pity Nineveh, that great city, in which are more than one hundred and twenty thousand persons who cannot discern between their right hand and their left..."

Jonah 4:11

Many times throughout our lives we may feel no one cares for us. I love that David wrote in the Psalms about the reality of human feelings of fear, rejection, disappointment, abandonment, sorrow of heart and anger. He also writes of God's faithfulness, mercy and care for us in the midst of these feelings as we read in Psalm 142:1-7:

"I cry out to the LORD with my voice;

With my voice to the LORD I make my supplication.
I pour out my complaint before Him;
I declare before Him my trouble.
When my spirit was overwhelmed within me,
Then You knew my path.
In the way in which I walk
They have secretly set a snare for me.
Look on my right hand and see,
For there is no one who acknowledges me;
Refuge has failed me;
No one cares for my soul.
I cried out to You, O LORD:
I said, "You are my refuge,
My portion in the land of the living.
Attend to my cry,
For I am brought very low;
Deliver me from my persecutors,
For they are stronger than I.
Bring my soul out of prison,
That I may praise Your name;
The righteous shall surround me,
For You shall deal bountifully with me."

God allows testing and trials to reveal what is hidden in our hearts, and He reveals to heal. Sometimes He leads us into the valley of the shadow of death that we may learn to trust Him, and there is where we are delivered from fear. His heart is not to harm, although it does hurt to walk through life with its suffering. He leads us through it (the valley) to take us to it (the promise). Through it all, He longs for us to know His heart and character. Walking through that valley is lonely, and sometimes, even horrifying. We find many opportunities and reasons to be offended by everything and everyone, even God. Much of what Jesus did and said offended people;

• Matthew 15:22-28: The Gentile woman He

referenced as a dog.

- Matthew 16:23: He addressed Peter and said "get behind Me Satan."
- Matthew 15:7-9,12: He called the Pharisees hypocrites; the disciples asked Him if He realized He had offended them.

God will often use an offense to reveal what is in our hearts to ourselves, which is a loving opportunity to be confronted with the truth. Once we see what is in our hearts, we then have the choice to repent, be healed, and walk in freedom and joy, or stay offended, be bitter, and walk in the bondage of a hurt and wounded spirit.

The ministry of *He Cares for Me* coaches believers as they walk through their valley into a beautiful place of joy and freedom. There have been hundres of people since the ministry was launched that can now declare as David did in Psalm 142:7:

"'...the righteous shall surround me and He has dealt bountifully with me."

When the Care Ministry team (the righteous) surrounds a person in need of forgiveness and freedom and prays for them, the Holy Spirit brings about deliverance and healing in a powerful way and does it bountifully (liberal in bestowing generous gifts, favors, a premium or reward, abundant supply).

Care Ministers are those who have been reached out to and then reach out their hand to lift up others.

Peter said, "If it is you, Lord, bid me come to you." Jesus called and Peter got out of the boat. He walked on water with Jesus while his eyes were on Him, but when Peter looked at the waves and the wind he began to sink. Jesus, having compassion, reached out His hand to keep Peter from going under.

Peter knew how to reach out his hand to one who needed help because he was the one Jesus reached out His hand to. Peter's own experience of the intervention of the Savior equipped him for the miracle God did through him in Acts 3:2-7,

"And a certain man lame from his mother's womb was carried, whom they laid daily at the gate of the temple which is called Beautiful, to ask alms from those who entered the temple; who, seeing Peter and John about to go into the temple, asked for alms. And fixing his eyes on him, with John, Peter said, 'Look at us.' So he gave them his attention, expecting to receive something from them. Then Peter said, 'Silver and gold I do not have, but what I do have I give you: In the name of Jesus Christ of Nazareth, rise up and walk.' And he took him by the right hand and lifted him up, and immediately his feet and ankle bones received strength."

Who are the Care Ministers: They are the redeemed sons and daughters of God, vessels of His amazing grace, and His healing love, living in the powerful truth that "whom the Son sets free is free indeed." We can only give what we have personally experienced of Holy Spirit's healing power through Christ's blood shed on the cross.

What we do: We teach biblical truths that have the potential to set at liberty the bruised and broken. Every individual is on the journey of healing and freedom but at different places of the journey. Some are at the beginning of sowing seed; some are at the watering place of what has already been sown and others are at the reaping the fruit stage of their journey. We coach believers to use the authority that Christ has given them.

How we coach: We coach using the Word of God and biblical healing prayer, leading believers to submit to the Father and resist the devil using both offensive and defensive truths. Our defense is our submission to His authority, and our offense is using our position of authority in Christ to discern, dismiss and dismantle the purposes and plans of the enemy. We don't counsel telling people what to do. We coach them to be obedient to what they already know to do- submit to God, resist the enemy. As coaches, we agree with them as they pray out loud using the authority of the blood and name of Christ over their own mind, will, emotions and life.

We coach and not counsel because we want to:

- Connect the individual to the life source, being God the Father, the Son and Holy Spirit.
- Train believers to use their authority and to lead themselves.
- Exhort believers to live from their position in Christ.

Where we minister: We minister under the covering of the local church, under the umbrella of Somebody Cares New England, and the ministry of *He Cares for Me.*

> "The authority Christ delegates to His own is intended to be exercised by disciples willing to accept revival in soul and behavior, as well as rebirth through forgiveness of sins."
>
> - Jack Hayford

Those who attend the Saturday Care Ministry training have two choices.

After training, they can grow forward under the leadership of their own local church Pastor to minister and care for the people within their own congregation. Our vision is to see the local church equipped to care for those in their own congregation.

Those in training do not serve as part of the Care Ministry Team, nor do they serve at the Healing Waters weekends, retreats or personal ministry appointments.

Then there are those called by God and blessed by their local pastor to serve in the ministry of *He Cares for Me* are then invited to continue training by attending the first Tuesday of every month as a part of their equipping to become a "Care Minister." During the first year of training they observe the deliverance ministry prayer sessions and serve as a part of the Ministry of Helps team, participating in intercession before the healing weekends and personal appointments as well as setting up, participating in the foot washing and caring for those who attend in whatever way needed.

If by the second year they have grown in their own life and are walking in humility and exercising their authority in their own life, they are interviewed to assess if the Lord is calling them to be a Care Minister.

In addition to Care Minister Training, we offer Kingston Cottage weekends, where we host marriage retreats, personal ministry and spa retreat, or personal ministry appointments for individuals that may need Care Ministry during the interim between Healing Waters weekends. The cottage is privately owned, and can be rented for small group church retreats and personal family vacations. All rental fees go directly to proprietor. For more information contact Martha Temple:

http://mtemplecottagerental.com

Or to view the cottage go to:

www.HeCaresForMe.org
and click the "Kingston Cottage" tab.

Identify

Open Doors

There are five entries into the human soul that have powerful potential to deface the image of God. Every human life is an original design and was knit and fashioned together in their mother's womb by the hand of God. The Father's heart and plan is to reveal Himself in and to mankind, who is made in His image. Since the beginning of the world and the Garden of Eden, Satan's evil wicked plan is to mar, scar and ultimately destroy every beautiful, healthy, gifted human being that is created by God Himself.

Each of the five entries is a door of opportunity Satan uses to cause man to sin:

- Iniquity: a violation, wicked act, sin, gross injustice or wickedness.

- Innocent: not involving evil intent or motive.

- Ignorant: lacking in knowledge or training; unlearned.

- Imputed: to attribute or ascribe something discreditable, dishonest or dishonorable to a person.

- Intentional: deliberate, on purpose, planned, with understanding

When coaching someone through deliverance prayer, I have found the Holy Spirit to be so gentle, compassionate, thorough and simple. His presence is so real that the person being ministered to testifies there is no anxiety only peace. There is no fear, only love. There is no shame, only acceptance. Freedom is not complicated, although walking through deliverance can often feel emotionally overwhelming.

We coach the person receiving ministry because they need to learn to walk themselves through future times of healing and deliverance using the keys and insights the Holy Spirit brings to them. We explain that the Care Minister will not do the hard work for them...but will do it with them, coaching them along the way. No one has more authority over your life than you do- not your parents, not your spouse, not your pastor, not your doctor. Jesus said in Luke 10:19-20,

"Behold, I give you the authority to trample on serpents and scorpions, and over all the power of the enemy, and nothing shall by any means hurt you. 20 Nevertheless do not rejoice in this, that the spirits are subject to you, but rather rejoice because your names are written in heaven."

And Luke 9:1-2,

"Then He called His twelve disciples together and gave them power and authority over all demons, and to cure diseases. He sent them to preach the kingdom of God and to heal the sick."

The challenge for most Christians is to understand Matthew 11:12,

"And from the days of John the Baptist until now the kingdom of heaven suffers violence, and the violent take it by force."

The warfare for the human soul is a violent one, and we need an aggressive, determined, fearless, confident attitude and mindset to win the battles for freedom.

"Therefore submit to God. Resist the devil and he will flee from you."

James 4:7

Most Christians pray polite, soft spoken, timid prayers. They are not very bold, passionate, confident or aggressive when resisting the devil. We would rather ask God to just take care of our part, which is to use our faith with authority. Somewhere there has been assumption, or maybe even teaching that discourages believers from taking their authority and casting out the enemy. When we don't walk in our spiritual authority, we are abdicating it to the adversary. The Bible states there are prayers that avail much in James 5:16,

"Confess your trespasses to one another, and pray for one another, that you may be healed. The effective, fervent prayer of a righteous man avails much."

When a person comes for prayer ministry and says, "I have no idea what is going on inside me, all I know is I am supposed to come for prayer," I always coach them to relax, and tell them that God wants to reveal the hidden things, so we are going to pray and invite the Holy Spirit to reveal the root issues that need to be addressed.

I love the simplicity of asking in faith, trusting and believing. He always answers. We have never once been without some kind of leading as to what direction to go that is either given to the person receiving ministry, or to the Care Minister.

Once He gives discernment, then we follow the simple format of disarming, dismissing, discharging, and decreeing and declaring, always giving thanks for His loving kindness toward us who believe. Following are the simple steps we apply to each root issue.

- **Discern:** Ask the Holy Spirit where the open door is. Care Ministers don't interview or dig for information. It has to come by revelation and discernment, which are gifts of the Holy Spirit. It is not a head thing, trying to think of what may be needed, it is a Spirit thing. The Bible says, "Ask and you shall receive." We don't have to work hard, we have to rest in the finished work of the cross.
- **Disarm:** The power of agreement we have had with the lies and break any covenants that were made with the lies.
- **Dismiss:** The assignment of hell that has been in your family blood line and had control.
- **Discharge:** Principalities and strip them of their authority, rendering them powerless.
- **Decree and Declare:** The truth of what God's Word says about you, the situation, and the person who wronged you.

Following is Elizabeth's testimony of deliverance from the spirit of rejection:

"One of the biggest problems I had before going into Healing Waters weekend was dealing with rejection. As a child I was rejected by my parents for not doing things correctly (cleaning, etc...)

As an adult I lived a performance life. I performed so I could get praised. Everything I did, I did with excellence, even before Christ. I had to be the best friend, the one who was down for all. Then, as a Christian

I had to always have the good grades, and pray the most, and be involved in all or any ministry opportunities.

When I went through Healing Waters, the Holy Spirit brought all this to light, and began to piece it all together and pinpoint the root.

I then chose to forgive my mom and take back what the enemy had stolen from me. What freedom I have experienced since then. Actually, two days ago, a top boss at my workplace came in where I was working and corrected me. Immediately, I felt the feelings of rejection and the old pattern of beating myself up tried to come back, but this time it was different.

I was able to speak the word of God with authority, plead the blood of Jesus over myself, and that familiar spirit left. Since Healing Waters weekend, I now walk in His authority to identify and nullify the works of the enemy. The wicked one comes, but now finds no place in me. I love God and I'm thankful for Jesus' love and freedom in my life. And that's what God does through Healing Waters Weekend."

He Cares For Me

Identity
The Matrix Of Human Life

I gained a lot of insight listening to the audio teaching by Arthur Burke "The Sound of Light."

"But You are He who took Me out of the womb; You made Me trust while on My mother's breasts. I was cast upon You from birth. From My mother's womb You have been My God. Be not far from Me, For trouble is near; For there is none to help."

Psalm 22:9-11

His teaching gives insight into the critical relationship between mother and child, and how the mental, emotional and spiritual state of the mother at the time of conception, delivery and raising her child during the first five years of his or her life, sets in place their sense of value and worth.

Mothers spend more time with the child in the first five years of their life, and mothers have a powerful impact on their children in the early stages of development even more so than their fathers.

"A child receives their sense of worth from their mother and a sense of identity from their father."

- Arthur Burke

"It is easier to build strong children than to repair broken men."

- Douglass Frederick

Although we draw a sense of identity from our earthly father, we draw our security in our identity from looking at His face. The eyes are the lamp of the soul, and when Christ is in the center of our soul, others can see Him in and through us.

"The light of the body is the eye."

Matthew 6:22

The LORD's light penetrates the human spirit, exposing every hidden motive.

"The spirit of a man is the lamp of the LORD, Searching all the inner depths of his heart."

Proverbs 20:27

"You are fearfully and wonderfully made from the earth."

Psalm 139:14

As stated before, most Christians live in fear and wonder why they were made and why they are on this earth.

- **Adam**
"The face of God was face to face with Adam – God breathed in his nostrils – mouth to nose. Face to face encounters give breath and life."

Genesis 2:7

- **Jacob**
"...For I have seen God face to face and my life is preserved."

Genesis 32:30

Jacob's character and name were changed to reflect the image of original intent.

- **Moses**

"So the Lord spoke to Moses face to face, as a man speaks to his friend..."

Exodus 33:11

- **Jesus**

"Sent them two by two before His face into every city and place where He Himself was about to go."

Luke 10:1

You can be busy with your hands doing the works of Jesus, and be running with your feet to preach the Gospel, but His face can only be revealed when we look at Him, when we are still in His presence and allow Him to look into our hearts and confront the wounds that have marred, marked and maimed us.

Only when we deal can we then heal. You may walk away from what you heard. You may walk away from what you said. It is not as easy to walk away from what you see. When you look at Him, His image changes the image of yourself and the image of how you see others.

"When You said, 'Seek My face,' My heart said to You, 'Your face, LORD, I will seek.'"

Psalm 27:8

The enemy wants to deface His face in your face. Deface means to mar the surface or appearance of; disfigure: to deface a wall by writing on it, to efface, obliterate, destroy or injure the surface of, as to make illegible or invalid. The enemy wants to deface the walls of your personality. In contrast, the Lord makes our face shine with His presence,

"I sought the LORD, and He heard me, And delivered

me from all my fears. They looked to Him and were radiant, And their faces were not ashamed."

Psalm 34:4-5

"The LORD bless you and keep you;
The LORD make His face shine upon you,
And be gracious to you;
The LORD lift up His countenance upon you,
And give you peace."

Numbers 6:24-26

Turn your face toward the Lord. Face your pain and let Him embrace you and kiss your face.

"When I was a child, I spoke as a child, I understood as a child, I thought as a child; but when I became a man, I put away childish things. For now we see in a mirror, dimly, but then face to face. Now I know in part, but then I shall know just as I also am known."

1 Corinthians 13:11-12

Let's revisit Acts 3 this time focusing on verses 4-5:

"Now Peter and John went up together to the temple at the hour of prayer, the ninth hour. And a certain man lame from his mother's womb was carried, whom they laid daily at the gate of the temple which is called Beautiful, to ask alms from those who entered the temple; who, seeing Peter and John about to go into the temple, asked for alms. And fixing his eyes on him, with John, Peter said, "Look at us." So he gave them his attention, expecting to receive something from them."

We can only give what we have received. Peter said, "Look at us." The reflection of the face of Jesus needs to be made real to the world, and He chooses to do it through us.

Many have been wounded in the womb. The physical, emotional and spiritual health of the mother, and her relationship with the father of the child, determine the well-being of the child within.

We need to recognize our personality strengths and weaknesses. Peter denied that he had character weaknesses. Jesus prophetically spoke to Peter that he was going to deny the Lord but Peter was not teachable, nor did he have a listening ear.

Jesus allowed Peter's heart to be exposed to him. It was at a coal fire in the courts of the place where Jesus was on trial that Peter denied the Lord three times. After the resurrection, Jesus recreated a similar scenario to give Peter the opportunity to face his failure at a coal fire on the beach.

Three times Jesus gave Peter an opportunity to make the three times he denied the Lord right. This time, Peter was teachable and had a listening ear. Peter faced his pain, received healing, and was restored.

I love how the Lord then used him to preach on the day of Pentecost. Regardless of the failures of our character and weaknesses of our personality, when we deal with our issues, we will be healed, and the Lord will use us to minister to others.

Abuse is defined as the following: to use wrongly or treat improperly, to abuse one's authority, to treat in a harmful, injurious, or offensive way, to speak insultingly, harshly, and unjustly to or about; revile; malign, to commit sexual assault upon, to deceive or mislead: wrong or improper use; misuse.

In the practical sense, abuse is when one human being

lords over and perpetrates another making them a victim subject to their words, ways and will. The abuser's goal is to control their victim for their own personal gain and pleasure with intention to delete the individual's personality and to gain the control needed to dominate and remake them into the image the abuser imposes on them.

When there is abuse of any kind, whether verbal, emotional, physical, sexual or spiritual, the very core of the matrix of one's soul is attacked. Abuse is a weapon Satan uses to twist, mar, scare and confuse a person's identity. Abuse confuses the human mind and heart about who God is, and what His true character is. It mangles (to injure severely, disfigure, or mutilate by cutting, slashing, or crushing) and tangles (to bring together into a mass of confused, interlaced or intertwined threads, strands, or other like parts) who you are, whose you are, why you were born and what your purpose is in this life. Abuse and neglect want to completely destroy and totally strike from us the DNA of who we really are as sons and daughters of the Creator God, and redefine, rewrite and reprogram us as orphans. Once we have lost the truth of who we are, we will then live our life with no compass, no purpose, and no God consciousness.

Following are a few adjectives that characterize what an orphan feels like:

Alone
Isolated
Unforgiven
Rejected
Insignificant
Unapproved
Abandoned
Low self-worth
Weak / Unstable

Not cared for
Low self-confidence
No friends
Unloved
Fear rules – cannot love
Forsaken
Not loveable
Shamed and wounded
No Father
Not part of a family
Not safe - insecure
No Mother
No home to go to
Cannot do good things
No future or hope

Jesus received his identity from the Father who sent him, although people could only identify Him by His earthly father, Joseph. He came from the bosom of the Father, and he returned to the Father. *(John 1:18, 16:28)*

The Father gives us identity, assignments, purpose, and destiny. The Son gives us companionship and friendship. He shows us the Father, and how to relate to God and man. The Holy Spirit gives us nurture, and comfort. He teaches and leads us into all the truth.

In the word identity, notice the I between the two t's. I use this simple analogy to remind myself that my identity is found in Christ, when on the cross, where He died for me between the two thieves, my life was redeemed and is now hidden in Him. That truth is the sum of where we receive our identity.

"If then you were raised with Christ, seek those things which are above, where Christ is, sitting at the right hand of God. Set your mind on things above, not on

things on the earth. For you died, and your life is hidden with Christ in God. When Christ who is our life appears, then you also will appear with Him in glory."
Colossians 3:1-4

When we live in the shame and pain of our sin, we hide our face from Him and from others. Our head hangs down, our hands hang down, our eyes look down, and eye contact makes us uncomfortable. It is more difficult to hide our true self and feelings when we are face to face.

God spoke to Moses as a friend face to face. Having meaningful conversations with another human being is foreign to most. We are much more comfortable blabbing all over Facebook from behind a computer than actually sorting through our hurt with intent to heal.

When I was a youth minister, I was shocked when talking to a member of the ministry team who was in their thirties.

I said, "You are very quiet and a challenge to get to know. I would like to get to know you better."

He thought for a minute, looked at me with a blank, funny stare and said, "It's a lot of work. I have assessed the situation and decided I don't want a relationship with you."

Well, alrighty then! I appreciated his honesty, and respected his wishes. I assessed the situation and decided he was too much work for me. Being around him was like pulling hens' teeth (of which they have none). I flipped it over and let it alone. Like the old Kenny Rogers song says,

"You've got to know when to hold 'em
Know when to fold 'em
Know when to walk away

And know when to run"

- The Gambler

Jesus is the discerner of all men's hearts and He gives us the wisdom to know who and who not to commit to. We need wisdom to choose our ministry relationships and kingdom friendships for we will give an account of where we invested our time, talent, and resources.

> *"But Jesus did not commit Himself to them, because He knew all men..."*
>
> John 2:24

It wasn't long before he felt led to leave youth ministry. In the many years that followed I never saw him involved in any area of church. He was a loner, liked being a loner and chose to stay a loner.

The beauty of His face is revealed to us as we look at His face. It is easy for us to be His hands and feet because that is the busy work of helping and serving others.

> *"Now it happened as they went that He entered a certain village; and a certain woman named Martha welcomed Him into her house. And she had a sister called Mary, who also sat at Jesus' feet and heard His word. But Martha was distracted with much serving, and she approached Him and said, 'Lord, do You not care that my sister has left me to serve alone? Therefore tell her to help me.' And Jesus answered and said to her, 'Martha, Martha, you are worried and troubled about many things. But one thing is needed, and Mary has chosen that good part, which will not be taken away from her.'"*
>
> Luke 10:38-42

We are comfortable with serving, but to take time

out of work to sit at His feet looking into His face is another story. That is where we find intimacy: into me see. It is when we look at Him and see His beauty and holiness, we see our need to stop blame shifting, minimizing, criticizing and denying, and start owning, confessing and repenting of our sin, we start to live in freedom.

I remember a time in my early days of walking with my Lord when I sat on the couch discouraged and angry. I was experiencing painful memories from my past. We all have them, you know, those things that are so painful and shameful that we can't bring ourselves to risk telling others for fear they would disown us, or deny us the opportunity to find healing by not reaching out a hand of compassion, hope and freedom. That would mean they would of have had to have walked that path of healing to help us, and so few are either willing to do so, or even know how to. As I sat there crying and complaining to the Lord that I had no one and nowhere that I felt safe, I clearly heard Him speak a word in my heart, "If I show you your pain will you trust me?" I was rather shocked by the thought, because I wasn't really expecting Him to speak to me and I was not sure of what would happen next.

The response from my heart was, "Yes Lord I trust You."

One by one, like a video, He revealed five incidences that wounded my soul as a young child. I forgave each person for the injustices done against me. As I repented and asked forgiveness for my part, I blessed and did not curse the abuser, asking for God's mercy and kindness to bring them to repentance. I asked for God to heal my broken heart and wounded emotions; asking the Holy Spirit to comfort and restore me.

I used my authority as a child of God to dismiss fear and shame and I declared that the power of the cross broke the curse and in the Name of Jesus, I was free!

You see, once you have a radical, life changing encounter with the power of His love that is able to deliver you from the guttermost and bring you into His uttermost, you too will be able to declare to the powers of darkness that had you bound, "I know in whom I have believed and I am fully persuaded that He is always ready, willing and able!"

When others see us do they see the radiance of His face in us?

"I sought the LORD, and He heard me, And delivered me from all my fears. They looked to Him and were radiant, And their faces were not ashamed. This poor man cried out, and the LORD heard him, And saved him out of all his troubles. The angel of the LORD encamps all around those who fear Him, And delivers them."

Psalm 34:4-7

Jesus already paid the price for our healing!

God was face to face with Adam when He breathed His breath into His nostrils, His mouth to Adam's nostrils. Since Jesus came face to face with the devil and the sin of humanity on the cross; we will come face to face with who we are in the fiery trials, and one day we will come face to face with Him when we see Him in all His glory!

We are all on the journey of healing. Every human being has emotional needs that can only be met through continual transformation by the power of the Holy Spirit. It is only as we look into the face of Jesus and let the Holy Spirit show us our own heart and brokenness will we reflect the face of Jesus to others. We can only get our source of joy, peace and righteousness from the One we look upon. We become what we behold.

> *"So when the LORD saw that he turned aside to look, God called to him from the midst of the bush and said, "Moses, Moses!" And he said, "Here I am." Then He said, "Do not draw near this place. Take your sandals off your feet, for the place where you stand is holy ground." Moreover He said, "I am the God of your father—the God of Abraham, the God of Isaac, and the God of Jacob." And Moses hid his face, for he was afraid to look upon God. And the LORD said: "I have surely seen the oppression of My people who are in Egypt, and have heard their cry because of their taskmasters, for I know their sorrows. So I have come down to deliver them out of the hand of the Egyptians, and to bring them up from that land to a good and large land, to a land flowing with milk and honey, to the place of the Canaanites and the Hittites and the Amorites and the Perizzites and the Hivites and the Jebusites. Now therefore, behold, the cry of the children of Israel has come to Me, and I have also seen the oppression with which the Egyptians oppress them. Come now, therefore, and I will send you to Pharaoh that you may bring My people, the children of Israel, out of Egypt." But Moses said to God, "Who am I that I should go to Pharaoh, and that I should bring the children of Israel out of Egypt?" So He said, "I will certainly be with you. And this shall be a sign to you that I have sent you: When you have brought the people out of Egypt, you shall serve God on this mountain." Then Moses said to God, "Indeed, when I come to the children of Israel and say to them, 'The God of your fathers has sent me to you,' and they say to me, 'What is His name?' what shall I say to them?" And God said to Moses, "I AM WHO I AM." And He said, "Thus you shall say to the children of Israel, 'I AM has sent me to you.'"*

Exodus 3: 4-14

"That which was from the beginning, which we have heard, which we have seen with our eyes, which we have looked upon, and our hands have handled, concerning the Word of life— the life was manifested, and we have seen, and bear witness, and declare to you that eternal life which was with the Father and was manifested to us— that which we have seen and heard we declare to you, that you also may have fellowship with us; and truly our fellowship is with the Father and with His Son Jesus Christ. And these things we write to you that your joy may be full."

1 John 1:1-4:

"After these things the Lord appointed seventy others also, and sent them two by two before His face into every city and place where He Himself was about to go. Then He said to them, 'The harvest truly is great, but the laborers are few; therefore pray the Lord of the harvest to send out laborers into His harvest'".

Luke 10:1-2

"So he answered and said, 'You shall love the LORD your God with all your heart, with all your soul, with all your strength, and with all your mind, and your neighbor as yourself.' And He said to him, 'You have answered rightly; do this and you will live.' But he, wanting to justify himself, said to Jesus, 'And who is my neighbor?'"

Luke 10:27-29

He Cares For Me

Iniquity

In The Beginning

The Hebrew word for iniquity; oehler, primarily denotes not an action, but the character of an action, and is so distinguished from sin (chaTTa'th). Iniquity is the tendency to sin, the bent toward sin, or the weakness of character to resist particular sin, whereas sin is the wicked act of iniquity in action. The New Testament translation of iniquity is the condition of one without law, or lawlessness.

The definition of sin is any immoral act or transgression against divine law.

God's divine law is found in the Ten Commandments. For the purpose of this chapter on iniquity we are looking at Exodus 20:1-6:

"And God spoke all these words: "I am the LORD your God, who brought you out of Egypt, out of the land of slavery. "You shall have no other gods before me. "You shall not make for yourself an image in the form of anything in heaven above or on the earth beneath or in the waters below. You shall not bow down to them or worship them; for I, the LORD your God, am a jealous God, punishing the children for the sin of the parents to the third and fourth generation of those who hate me, but showing love to a thousand generations of those who love me and keep my commandments."

To make it clear and simple, here is my paraphrased rendition of the root and fruit of iniquity:

"I am the Lord your God, I am your deliverer. You are no longer a slave but a son. Live like my son, be like Me, your Father. Don't put yourself under the rulership of lesser gods for they intend to make you their slave. Do not allow those lesser gods to make, form, or forge an image of anything in this world in your mind. Do not give them a place in your mind to make a nest (a home) in your thoughts. Once a nest has been made of their image of you, the fowls of the air will come to live there and produce their offspring. Do not be subservient to the images; do not let them have control over your mind because you become the image of what your thoughts lead you to believe in your heart."

These lesser gods are determined to have complete ownership of your soul. They want to remove My image in you and replace it with their image of you. Don't allow them access to your soul or obey them. They want to bring disaster on future generations by gaining lordship over you. They want to use you to destroy your children and your children's children even to the fourth generation. They want your heart as their breeding ground to sow hate; not only in your heart, but in the heart of your children, so your children will hate and blame Me for your sinful lifestyle.

My heart's' intention is to demonstrate My love to you and your children, even to one thousand generations. I am going to demonstrate that love through My Son, Christ Jesus, so that all of those in future generations will see and know that I love them. When they respond to My love and love Me in return, I intend to bless them in every way, if they will only listen and obey my commands.

Because man (Adam) was not willing to obey God's command (law) and chose to disobey, there was another law set in motion (action). This law is referred to in scripture as the law of sowing and reaping. Every act or action sets in motion another act or action, both in your own life, and the future life of your offspring. Transgression of the law makes us transgressors.

David wrote Psalm 51 after committing adultery with Bathsheba. Seeking forgiveness and restoration, he acknowledges he was conceived in his mother's sin and father's iniquity.

"Have mercy upon me, O God, According to Your lovingkindness; According to the multitude of Your tender mercies, Blot out my transgressions. Wash me thoroughly from my iniquity, And cleanse me from my sin. For I acknowledge my transgressions, And my sin is always before me. Against You, You only, have I sinned, And done this evil in Your sight—That You may be found just when You speak, And blameless when You judge. Behold, I was brought forth in iniquity, And in sin my mother conceived me. Behold, You desire truth in the inward parts, And in the hidden part You will make me to know wisdom. Purge me with hyssop, and I shall be clean; Wash me, and I shall be whiter than snow. Make me hear joy and gladness, That the bones You have broken may rejoice. Hide Your face from my sins, And blot out all my iniquities. Create in me a clean heart, O God, And renew a steadfast spirit within me. Do not cast me away from Your presence, And do not take Your Holy Spirit from me. Restore to me the joy of Your salva-

tion, And uphold me by Your generous Spirit. Then I will teach transgressors Your ways, And sinners shall be converted to You. Deliver me from the guilt of bloodshed, O God, The God of my salvation, And my tongue shall sing aloud of Your righteousness. O Lord, open my lips, And my mouth shall show forth Your praise. For You do not desire sacrifice, or else I would give it; You do not delight in burnt offering. The sacrifices of God are a broken spirit, A broken and a contrite heart—These, O God, You will not despise."

Psalm 51:1-17

The iniquity of sexual sin was already at work in David's blood line. The first chapter of Matthew lists David's lineage from Abraham to Jesus. Looking back at least four generations is Rahab the harlot. Iniquity and the sin of lawlessness is in every family bloodline because our ancestral roots go back to Adam in the Garden of Eden. He was given the tree of life and every tree in the garden to eat except one, the tree of the knowledge of good and evil. The only fruit he was commanded not to eat, he ate.

God leaves the choice to us of what we want to feed on. All through the ages, the sum total of life can be boiled down to one choice- to obey and live, or to disobey and die. I am not talking about death of the physical body. I am referencing another death, which I call it "living dead." This death is played out in the law of sowing and reaping. Like a seed, we plant, water, nurture, protect and reproduce our sinful DNA nature in another human life, reproducing death in our relationships, health, finances and future.

The following is taken from an article Billy Graham wrote, entitled "The Mystery of Lawlessness and the Tide of Evil." The Bible teaches that God did not create evil and sin, but that somewhere in the past it began with "Lucifer, son of the morning" *(Isaiah 14:12)*, rebelling against God.

People are born to sin "as surely as sparks fly upward" *(Job 5:7)*. The seeds of evil are propagated from parent to child, each little one bringing into the world, as his spiritual inheritance, a propensity for evil that mingles with all his propensities for good. Each new life seems to bring a fresh contribution to the already abundant growth of evil. It is a mere germ at first, but unfolds speedily, and grows with the growth of the child.

What are its consequences? The Bible tells us that all who are guilty of sin will be judged and eventually banished from the Kingdom of God. How mysterious are the chastisements and judgments that fall upon us in this life and in the life to come.

The Bible teaches that our sins will find us out, "for whatever a man sows, that he will also reap" *(Galatians 6:7)*. In this life, our sins will find us out in ruined character, broken homes, confused minds, disillusioned hearts, and empty souls.

There are many mysteries about it all, but God has revealed to us that sin is a transgression of the law and a "missing of the mark."

- We are told what sin is.
- We are warned about its terrible and tragic consequences.
- We are told to flee the wrath of God.
- We are told to repent of sin before it is too late.

"I acknowledged my sin to you and did not cover up my iniquity. I said, 'I will confess my transgressions to the LORD.'"

Psalm 32:5

In this verse, "sin," "iniquity," and "transgression" are all mentioned. Basically each of these words communicates the same idea, evil lawlessness.

"Blessed is he whose transgression is forgiven, Whose sin is covered. Blessed is the man to whom the LORD does not impute iniquity, And in whose spirit there is no deceit. When I kept silent, my bones grew old Through my groaning all the day long. For day and night Your hand was heavy upon me; My vitality was turned into the drought of summer. Selah I acknowledged my sin to You, And my iniquity I have not hidden. I said, "I will confess my transgressions to the LORD," And You forgave the iniquity of my sin. Selah For this cause everyone who is godly shall pray to You In a time when You may be found; Surely in a flood of great waters They shall not come near him. You are my hiding place; You shall preserve me from trouble; You shall surround me with songs of deliverance."

Psalm 32:1-7

"For the mystery of lawlessness is already at work; only He who now restrains will do so until He is taken out of the way. And then the lawless one will be revealed, whom the Lord will consume with the breath of His mouth and destroy with the brightness of His coming. The coming of the lawless one is according to the working of Satan, with all power, signs, and lying wonders, and with all unrighteous deception among those who perish, because they did not receive the love of the truth, that they might be saved. And for this reason God will send them strong delusion, that they should believe the lie, that they all may be condemned who did not believe the truth but had pleasure in unrighteousness."

2 Thessalonians 2: 7-12

Innocent

Causing Little Ones To Stumble

I grew up in the generation that said, "children are to be seen and not heard." In my own terms, children may be present, but they did not have a voice. Their thoughts and feelings were not important. Children were told what to think, how to feel, what to eat, and how to dress. We were not taught life skills like how to reason, process thoughts or feelings, find solutions, deal with disappointments, or bring closure to painful experiences.

I can remember hearing the words, "What are you crying for? I'll give you something to cry about." We were sent outside to play early in the morning, called in for lunch, and sent back outside until supper. In the early evening daylight of spring, summer, and fall, we were sent to bed, which felt so unfair, but it was, "the way life was."

Children interpret negative life experiences as "their fault", drawing subconscious conclusions that who they are at the very core of their being is "wrong." Too often, the very ones they look to for affirmation cannot be found. Left to themselves, they conclude, "I have no worth, no value, no purpose, and it's my fault that life is so hard."

It was in the early formative vulnerable years of my life that the enemy found an opening to strike deep wounds in my soul. Being left alone outdoors for long periods of time with no adult presence or supervision opened the door to the older neighborhood kids and a babysitter who exposed my innocence to vile conduct and deeds.

I can remember being about five to six years old and having a tender heart toward Jesus. There was a picture of Him surrounded by little children in my bedroom over my white wicker chair. It was in that room that I have very vivid memories of being harshly disciplined by both my parents and looking at that picture feeling like this gentle, kind man was watching yet doing nothing to prevent it. I felt extremely violated by my parents and by God. Even as a child, I knew the punishment did not warrant the crime of "not cleaning my room." I saw the Jesus in the picture with other children like the Jesus in my life, present but silent, distant and uncommitted to my care, protection or well being.

God's will and intention for adults, parents, teachers, police and caregivers who have been entrusted with the life of a child is made known to those who look for it. Do not cause a little one to stumble, provoke not your children to wrath, and bring up a child in the care, nurture and admonition of the Lord.

I am so grateful for my Heavenly Father who is forever reaching out to the soul of every living being to turn our hearts toward Him and to one another.

> *"He will also go before Him in the spirit and power of Elijah, 'to turn the hearts of the fathers to the children,' and the disobedient to the wisdom of the just, to make ready a people prepared for the Lord."*
> Luke 1:17

Before my heart had been captured by God's love, I can remember saying that I wasn't particularly fond of children. To know me then and to know me now, you would not believe that I could have ever felt that way at one time. Because the wounds of my childhood are healed, I am mad-crazy in love with kids of all ages! Children were never my issue: my own childhood pain was my issue.

"Bless the beasts and the children; for in this world
they have no voice, they have no choice.
Light their way when the darkness surrounds them
give them love let it shine all around them.
Give them shelter from a storm,
keep them safe, keep them warm, the children..."

-"Bless the Beasts and the Children"
written by Barry De Vorzon and Perry Botkin, Jr

I believe the words of this song are the cry of the Father's heart for His children. When I look around at the children in the world today, I am overwhelmed by the trauma, drama, devastation and pain they live in. Working in the inner city with "Somebody Cares New England" outreaches and pastoring Community Christian Fellowship, I find my heart often grieved for the children.

One hot summer day, outside the window of our church, a very young distressed mom was frantically dragging her three little ones down the street. The four year old revolted and sat down on the sidewalk screaming, "I can't walk anymore." As the mom began to scream and swear at him, it was obvious that at any moment this situation was going to turn abusive.

My heart was wrenched with sadness for them all. I see it every day; abused, chemically dependent, and emotionally frenzied young women are having babies. They are not capable of caring for themselves, let alone their precious children.

I stepped out on the side walk calmly offering to help.

She yelped, "I have no one to help me and my baby is sick with a high fever. I have to get her to the hospital and I have two miles left to go, and this one decides he can't walk anymore!"

I said, "I can help you if you will let me. I am a grand-mother with two car seats in my car, and I can give you a ride to the hospital and back."

I invited her into our air conditioned café, and had one of our volunteers get them all a Popsicle while I got the car from the rear parking lot. As we drove to the hospital, the kids were quiet and happy to have a ride and a Popsicle.

The mom had calmed down and with tears of grati-tude said, "No one has ever offered to help me, I feel so all alone."

Good sense would tell you, that this is not your issue, mind your own business, turn away, turn up the music, you can't fix this problem.

God sense is different. He cares and demonstrates His care through His body, the Church.

So far we have looked at many forms of abuse, but the following testimony reveals the powerful impact a parent has on their child when the parent is in crisis. They discon-nect from the emotional and physical needs of their child. Although they are physically present, they are emotional absent. This creates a sense of insecurity in the child. As children often do, they will blame themselves for not being able to make their parent feel better. Performing to make them happy. Such was the testimony of Eternity before at-tending Healing Waters:

"This past weekend I attended Healing Waters, and my life was completely changed. I got wrecked by the Father's love for me. The Holy Spirit revealed things to me; the things I had gone through as a child that I tried to just forget about.

I never realized that the painful loss was a root to a lot of questions I had in my life. One in particular was when I was eight years old, my little two month old sister died in her daycare. I couldn't understand her death, so I just got over it.

As the years went on, my Mom was very abrasive emotionally and physically. She was completely detached from our lives as kids. I didn't understand why my Mom was not present mentally. Going through "Healing Waters", the Lord showed me the root my rejection was my Mom not being understanding and the detachment was her way of grieving.

18 years later, sadly, she is still grieving. I have never been able to tell my Mom I love her without the emptiness I felt in my heart as the words left my lips. I was coached in Healing Waters to forgive my Mom, to bless her, and take authority over my childhood losses and over the spirit of rejection.

After ministry, I spoke to my Mom and at the end of our conversation I could genuinely say "I love you." I felt so whole.

As a result of my mom's detachment, I lacked confidence, and carried guilt in my heart all these years, but God showed me it was never my fault.

I am so free today, and I am excited to grow to be one

of those who would lead others into their freedom! Thank you, He Cares for Me, for taking the time to care for me. :)"

Ignorant
Of The Devil's Devices

In order for the devil to take advantage of us, we have to give him the authority to do so. Through our ignorance, we give him the advantage. Paul writes in 2 Corinthians 2:11:

".... Lest Satan should take advantage of us; for we are not ignorant of his devices."

I believe two of the greatest weapons of the devil to bring a snare against the life of a believer are offense and fear.

"Be angry, and do not sin": do not let the sun go down on your wrath, nor give place to the devil.

Ephesians 4:26-27

"The fear of man brings a snare, But whoever trusts in the LORD shall be safe."

Proverbs 29:25

God's plan when He created mankind was for man to rule and reign with Him. When we are offended and fearful, we surrender our authority to the enemy.

"Then God said, 'Let Us make man in Our image, according to Our likeness; let them have dominion over the fish of the sea, over the birds of the air, and over the cattle, over all the earth and over every creeping

thing that creeps on the earth.' So God created man in His own image; in the image of God He created him; male and female He created them. Then God blessed them, and God said to them, 'Be fruitful and multiply; fill the earth and subdue it; have dominion over the fish of the sea, over the birds of the air, and over every living thing that moves on the earth.'"

Genesis 1:26-28

"The LORD God planted a garden eastward in Eden, and there He put the man whom He had formed. And out of the ground the LORD God made every tree grow that is pleasant to the sight and good for food. The tree of life was also in the midst of the garden, and the tree of the knowledge of good and evil."

Genesis 2:8-9

"Then the LORD God took the man and put him in the Garden of Eden to tend and keep it. And the LORD God commanded the man, saying, 'Of every tree of the garden you may freely eat; but of the tree of the knowledge of good and evil you shall not eat, for in the day that you eat of it you shall surely die.'"

Genesis 2:15-16

God placed man in the garden, and gave him everything except one thing. With only one restriction to not eat of the fruit of the tree of the knowledge of good and evil. There were two opportunities for problems. The first, God gave man a choice. Second, there was a jealous fallen angel named Diablos, the devil, who wanted the highest place of rule, the place that belonged to the Creator God. This fallen angel who once had a place in heaven over worship, lost his place because of rebellion and, was cast down to the earth where his mantra is, "Worship me and I will give you all the kingdoms of this world."

"How you are fallen from heaven, O Lucifer, son of the morning! How you are cut down to the ground, You who weakened the nations! For you have said in your heart: 'I will ascend into heaven, I will exalt my throne above the stars of God; I will also sit on the mount of the congregation On the farthest sides of the north, I will ascend above the heights of the clouds, I will be like the Most High.' Yet you shall be brought down to Sheol, To the lowest depths of the Pit. "Those who see you will gaze at you, And consider you, saying: 'Is this the man who made the earth tremble, Who shook kingdoms, Who made the world as a wilderness And destroyed its cities, Who did not open the house of his prisoners?'"

Isaiah 14:2-17

The devil has no new tricks. Although they are ancient, they are still effective in ensnaring the fallen nature of man.

Christians live their life doing the dance of fear. Fear will always keep you out of the blessings and favor of God. As a pastor, dancing with the "fear of man" is a non-negotiable. As already stated in Proverbs 29:26, the fear of man is a snare, a trap, an assignment to destroy our very life, as well as our call to ministry.

Church life presents lots of opportunities to dance with fear because we are always dealing with fearful people. Many of them are angry, broken, confused, hurt, disappointed, difficult people; People with authority issues, money issues, and trust issues who gather on a Sunday to worship God. They confess a love for God but they don't play well with others who are a part of God's family. I have found that people are people. Those who have accepted Christ have the exact same character and behaviors as those who don't know Christ.

105

So what makes the difference? Sanctification, which is a work of the Holy Spirit in the life of a surrendered believer who is willing to die daily, take up their cross and follow the teachings of Christ.

The Lord allowed several instrumental opportunities for me to face and conquer the fear of man. There was only one choice for me to make, "do, or die". It was a setup, and I decided it was high time to end the dance, conquer the fear of man that had been tormenting me my whole life.

When I was sent out by my home church in Lowell, Massachusetts, to plant Community Christian Fellowship in Haverhill, Massachusetts, there was a church that was supporting me monthly as a missionary. Because we were a church plant, there wasn't a budget set for even a stipend, never mind a salary, for the pastor. I was fully prepared to answer the call of God regardless.

I was so grateful to receive monthly support for almost two years...then the test came.

The church building we were using for our services was suddenly no longer available for our use, and we were given a time frame for when we had to be out. The reason for our eviction was the overseers of the building could not allow me to preach about the sanctity of marriage as one man, and one woman in the same building where they performed same sex marriages. In the same exact time frame, the church that was supporting me as a missionary to my city, notified me of terminating the monthly support. In a moment everything changed, no building, no support.

The Lord giveth and the Lord taketh away, blessed be the name of the Lord! I knew it was a test and praise His Name...I passed!

We ended up renting three store fronts in the same neighborhood as the church building we were asked to leave, which is on the city block where we had been praying for many years. Yay God! What was the end of support and a building space, became the beginning of a whole new chapter. Not only in my life, but in the life of the church.

Shortly following our move, one of our staff members began to show signs of unhealthy attitudes toward me and the ministry. They disagreed with the move into storefronts, and began to act out in very obvious ways. The church bookkeeper brought to the elders' attention that this leader was withholding tithes, and had been for some time.

It is not my custom to question whether someone tithes or not, but when it comes to leadership, the pastor needs to know if the leaders are obedient to Scripture, especially when they are mentoring others. I had no idea the amount this person tithed until this point. The elders had a meeting to talk to this leader to assess the situation and to find ways to reconcile what the offense was. Unfortunately, we were never able to do so.

If there is one thing I have learned through it all, "you can live without each other, but you can never replace each other."

I chuckle when my pastor Rafael Najem says, "Some are a blessing when they come and some are a blessing when they go." There is a sadness that the whole congregation has to deal with whenever a person leaves, whether it is for good, or not so good, reasons.

This situation was yet another test for me to face the fear of man and the fear of disapproval. This person's tithe was actually one quarter of our church's monthly income.

I knew it was God who called us to birth the church, and now God was going to have to prove Himself as the provider and sustainer of His baby.

I was not going to allow someone to control my obedience to the will of God.

Within a very short amount of time, a prophet, to whom a mutual friend had given my number, called me regarding a ministry issue, and began to prophetically speak to me:

> "The Lord says that you have passed the test. The fear of man has been broken and because you kept true to My word and My will I am going to bless you!"

We don't get to choose the test or the people used for the test, but we do get to choose how we respond.

> *"I called on the LORD in distress; The LORD answered me and set me in a broad place. The LORD is on my side; I will not fear. What can man do to me? The LORD is for me among those who help me; Therefore I shall see my desire on those who hate me. It is better to trust in the LORD Than to put confidence in man. It is better to trust in the LORD Than to put confidence in princes."*
>
> Psalm 118:5-9

Intentional

We Know It's Wrong And Do It Anyway

All sin is harmful and hurtful to us and to others, but intentional sin is a bit more dangerous. This type of sin comes with consequences that often have a very high price, because we know better.

James 4:17 in the VOICE translation says:

"So if you know the right way to live and ignore it, it is sin—plain and simple."

There are two Bible characters who come to mind whenever I think of intentional sin. Both of them suffered terrible consequences. Before we jump in, let me just say, all have sinned and fallen short. Every one of us, given the right circumstances, have the same potential to do exactly what these two men did, so let's not be too hard on them and judge them harshly. After all, we all need mercy! The first one we will look at is King David in 2 Samuel 11:1-3:

"It happened in the spring of the year, at the time when kings go out to battle, that David sent Joab and his servants with him, and all Israel; and they destroyed the people of Ammon and besieged Rabbah. But David remained at Jerusalem. Then it happened one evening that David arose from his bed and walked on the roof of the king's house. And from the roof he saw a woman bathing, and the woman was very beauti-

ful to behold. So David sent and inquired about the woman. And someone said, 'Is this not Bathsheba, the daughter of Eliam, the wife of Uriah the Hittite?'"

David knew that he was supposed to be on the battle-field with his men but instead he lingered behind, alone, finding himself in the heat of temptation. Instead of turning away from the temptation by turning toward God, he lingered, looked, and lost the battle against the flesh. Ultimately, it cost Bathsheba's husband Uriah his life and cost King David the death of his infant son.

All it takes for evil to triumph is for us to open the intentional door of the flesh to give birth to sin. As James 1:12-15 says:

"Blessed is the man who endures temptation; for when he has been approved, he will receive the crown of life which the Lord has promised to those who love Him. Let no one say when he is tempted, 'I am tempted by God'; for God cannot be tempted by evil, nor does He Himself tempt anyone. But each one is tempted when he is drawn away by his own desires and enticed. Then, when desire has conceived, it gives birth to sin; and sin, when it is full-grown, brings forth death."

As Christians, we can mentally assent to the truth that we are in a spiritual war. It is not enough to just know it, we must actively engage in spiritual warfare with the wisdom and weapons that God provides for us, as stated in Ephesians 6:10-18:

"Finally, my brethren, be strong in the Lord and in the power of His might. Put on the whole armor of God, that you may be able to stand against the wiles of the devil. For we do not wrestle against flesh and blood,

but against principalities, against powers, against the rulers of the darkness of this age, against spiritual hosts of wickedness in the heavenly places. Therefore take up the whole armor of God, that you may be able to withstand in the evil day, and having done all, to stand. Stand therefore, having girded your waist with truth, having put on the breastplate of righteousness, and having shod your feet with the preparation of the gospel of peace; above all, taking the shield of faith with which you will be able to quench all the fiery darts of the wicked one. And take the helmet of salvation, and the sword of the Spirit, which is the word of God; praying always with all prayer and supplication in the Spirit, being watchful to this end with all perseverance and supplication for all the saints— and for me, that utterance may be given to me, that I may open my mouth boldly to make known the mystery of the gospel, for which I am an ambassador in chains; that in it I may speak boldly, as I ought to speak."

Our war isn't against people, but if we don't keep our eyes on the Lord, it becomes about people and we become engaged in a struggle with the flesh.

The following story is about a woman who had been a Christian for many years. She was raised by a godly mother, and was not only taught as a child what was right, but was also shown what right looked like. As an adult, she even served in a local church as a ministry leader for many years.

Thank God she attended the "Healing Waters" weekend, and His goodness brought her to repentance. He gave her yet another opportunity to be obedient. Priscilla's testimony is as follows:

"I was raised by a principled woman, a woman who

knew how to love, give, and forgive. When it came to forgiveness, I did not understand why she forgave my father while I was angry at my father for dying. When my mother had to work hard to make ends meet, I blamed my father. When I couldn't get what I wanted, either for school trips, or simply just not having a person to call father, again I blamed my father. There were so many things I wanted to ask him. I was just three years old when he passed away. How he lived his life was not something to write home about, even though he was a great provider and educator (from a worldly point of view).

For every unfortunate thing I experienced as a child, I blamed my father. My mother used to talk me out of it and even tried using Scripture to redirect my heart and mind, but I was not willing to let go of my anger.

I would go to church, get involved in church activities and all, but that anger was a personal issue between me and my father, and I did not want God to deal with it.

My anger towards my father was not something I kept to myself; I talked about it and even warned those who mentored me never to touch that department. Whoever tried to talk or disciple me out of my anger, I would get angry with, and I declared that if my anger towards my father was the road to hell, then so be it. I will meet him there and deal with him; I was willing to sacrifice my salvation. Then came the Healing Waters weekend, something I had never ever experienced before. The Word was preached, hearts were touched, and God was doing His thing.

On that Saturday night, my heart was being worked on, but my head was fighting a do or die battle.

I drew a battle line, and I said, "God do your thing, but do not try to change my heart and feelings towards my father because I will not change."

I wrestled with this feeling over and over and the more I sat in the session, the more I felt like my heart was being changed and at some point I wanted to walk out, but I heard His voice saying, "The Cross, Jesus on the cross. He died for you so you may live. Did He die in vain? Surrender so you may be healed."

I do not know how I got up, but I found myself standing in front of the Care Minister, crying, saying, "I am willing to forgive once and for all and never look back."

That was a day of victory for me. The anger that I kept in for so many years, on that day the walls came down. Free at last, free indeed, I feel it, walk it and I am not afraid to declare it because I walk in His authority with no fear because I am FREE!"

What an amazing testimony. Intentional sin is also seen clearly in the life of Samson.

"And the Angel of the LORD appeared to the woman and said to her, "Indeed now, you are barren and have borne no children, but you shall conceive and bear a son. Now therefore, please be careful not to drink wine or similar drink, and not to eat anything unclean. For behold, you shall conceive and bear a son. And no razor shall come upon his head, for the child shall be a Nazirite to God from the womb; and he shall begin to deliver Israel out of the hand of the Philistines." So the woman came and told her husband, saying, "A Man of God came to me, and His countenance

*was like the countenance of the Angel of God,
very awesome; but I did not ask Him where He was
from, and He did not tell me His name. And He said
to me, 'Behold, you shall conceive and bear a son.
Now drink no wine or similar drink, nor eat anything
unclean, for the child shall be a Nazirite to God from
the womb to the day of his death.'"*

Judges 13:3-7 NIV

Samson was called by God to be a Nazarite from his mother's womb, but Samson never submitted to the call on his life. He knew what a Nazarite calling was. There were three things in particular: Not to cut his hair as a sign of covenant, not to drink wine and not to touch anything dead.

Samson loved to play games with the enemy, though it caught up with him when he ended up being seduced by Delilah, his head was shaved and he was captured by the Philistines. They gouged out his eyes and mocked him and his God. Nonetheless God stayed true to His promise to Hannah and did use Samson even in his death, to bring about a great deliverance for the children of Israel.

Have you noticed that in our day and age, despite the information we are given regarding the dangers of sexually transmitted diseases, the "Say no to Drugs" programs, and all the warnings of heroin and crack addictions, how horrific the number of premature deaths are among our young? Every person who chooses to willfully and knowingly commit a crime and sinful act is causing hurt and harm to themselves, their families and society.

We must guard our hearts and heed the warning, lest we become like those that were warned and fell away in Hebrews 3:7-15,

"Today, if you will hear His voice,

Do not harden your hearts as in the rebellion,
In the day of trial in the wilderness,
Where your fathers tested Me, tried Me, And saw My
works forty years.
Therefore I was angry with that generation,
And said, 'They always go astray in their heart,
And they have not known My ways.'
So I swore in My wrath, 'They shall not enter My
rest.'" Beware, brethren, lest there be in any of you an
evil heart of unbelief in departing from the living God;
but exhort one another daily, while it is called 'Today,'
lest any of you be hardened through the deceitfulness
of sin. For we have become partakers of Christ if we
hold the beginning of our confidence steadfast to the
end, while it is said:
'Today, if you will hear His voice,
Do not harden your hearts as in the rebellion.'"

When we intentionally sin, we become those who resist the truth and become disapproved concerning the faith. As in 2 Timothy 3:7-8,

"Always learning and never able to come to the knowledge of the truth. Now as Jannes and Jambres resisted Moses, so do these also resist the truth: men of corrupt minds, disapproved concerning the faith; but they will progress no further, for their folly will be manifest to all, as theirs also was."

"Sin will take you farther than you want to go, keep you longer than you want to stay and cost you more than you want to pay."

- Anonymous

He Cares For Me

Imputed

Sinned Against By Another

I love the story of David and Mephibosheth as it describes our story beautifully, that is the ones who have been redeemed. It is found in 2 Samuel 4:4:

"Jonathan, Saul's son, had a son who was lame in his feet. He was five years old when the news about Saul and Jonathan came from Jezreel; and his nurse took him up and fled. And it happened, as she made haste to flee, that he fell and became lame. His name was Mephibosheth.

Now David said, 'Is there still anyone who is left of the house of Saul, that I may show him kindness for Jonathan's sake?' And there was a servant of the house of Saul whose name was Ziba. So when they had called him to David, the king said to him, 'Are you Ziba?' He said, 'At your service!' Then the king said, 'Is there not still someone of the house of Saul, to whom I may show the kindness of God?' And Ziba said to the king, 'There is still a son of Jonathan who is lame in his feet.'' So the king said to him, 'Where is he?' And Ziba said to the king, 'Indeed he is in the house of Machir the son of Ammiel, in Lo Debar.' Then King David sent and brought him out of the house of Machir the son of Ammiel, from Lo Debar. Now when Mephibosheth the son of Jonathan, the son of Saul, had come to David, he fell on his face and prostrated himself. Then David said, 'Mephi-bosheth?' And he answered, 'Here is your servant!' So David said to him, 'Do not fear, for I will surely show you kindness for Jonathan your father's sake, and will restore to you all the land of Saul your grand-father; and you shall eat bread at my table continual-ly.' Then he bowed himself, and said, 'What is your servant, that you should look upon such a dead dog as I?' And the king called to Ziba, Saul's servant, and said to him, 'I have given to your master's son all that belonged to Saul and to all his house. You therefore, and your sons and your servants, shall work the land for him, and you shall bring in the harvest, that your master's son may have food to eat. But Mephibosheth your master's son shall eat bread at my table always.' Now Ziba had fifteen sons and twenty servants. Then Ziba said to the king, 'According to all that my lord the king has commanded his servant, so will your servant do.' 'As for Mephibosheth,' said the king, 'he shall eat at my table like one of the king's sons.' Me-phibosheth had a young son whose name was Micha. And all who dwelt in the house of Ziba were servants of Mephibosheth. So Mephibosheth dwelt in Jerusa-lem, for he ate continually at the king's table. And he was lame in both his feet."

2 Samuel 9:1-13

It is important to know the meaning behind the names in this story to see the powerful redemptive love of God. David's name means beloved, which is a type and shadow of an Old Testament picture of Jesus Christ as our Beloved. Jonathan means Jehovah has given, or the gift of God. Jon-athan was a gift from God to David as his friend. Jonathan's son's name Mephibosheth, has both definition and bibli-cal meaning. The definition of his name is the mouth of shame. The biblical meaning is exterminating the idol or contender with Baal.

When King David found Mephibosheth, he was living in Lo-Debar, located in Gilead, which was considered a ghetto town in biblical times. The name is a derivative of Debir which means "no pasture, no word and no communication."

When Mephibosheth was five years old, his grandfather, King Saul, died. It was Old Testament custom to kill all the relatives of the former king when the new king came into power. Fearing for Mephibosheth's life, his nurse maid ran to hide and fell on him, crushing both of his feet, and causing him to be crippled.

Many years later, as an adult, Mephibosheth heard that King David, who was his father Jonathan's best friend, wanted to see him. This was not good news. In Mephibosheth's eyes, he was an enemy of David, so he did not want to be found. In his mind, the only thing he could expect from David would be judgment, punishment and death.

Instead of what Mephibosheth expected, King David showed loving kindness to his friend Jonathan's son. The king brought him from Lo-debar, gave him a place at the king's table, and restored to Mephibosheth everything he had lost. Once known as the mouth of shame, he was now known as the Baal idol smasher. Way to go God! The weak one, the crippled one, and the shameful one is an idol smasher- boom shaka laka!

What a beautiful picture of the Gospel, the Good News! We were lamed and shamed by sin. We deserved punishment and death, yet Jesus took upon Himself all our sin and shame on the cross. Now, instead of what we deserved, we get mercy, forgiveness, blessing and restoration of all that was lost. Then the Lord anoints us to set others free! Is it any wonder the enemy fights so hard to keep us in the prison house of bitterness, judgments and unforgiveness?

John Arnott's book, "The Importance of Forgiveness," is in my opinion, a must read for every Christian. It addresses the issue of forgiveness and how it effects us. We must learn to forgive.

When we are the sinner, and the Holy Spirit reminds us of it, we want mercy, don't we?

Yet, when we are sinned against, we cry out for justice and often become bitter. We don't realize this is a subtle trap of the enemy. If satan can get us demanding justice, then he will be legally entitled to bring into our lives all the reaping and punishment we deserve.

> *"If the spirit of the ruler rises against you, Do not leave your post; For conciliation pacifies great offenses.There is an evil I have seen under the sun, As an error proceeding from the ruler..."*
>
> Ecclesiastes 10:4-5

The definition of conciliation is a method of helping the parties in a dispute to reach agreement, to part peaceably, to overcome the hostility.

The story of Jacob and Laban brings understanding and insight into how the children of God are to respond to imputed sin. Because of iniquity, there is a theme in families of the same tendencies, weaknesses and sins that can be identified from one generation to the next. Before looking at the story of Jacob, we need to go back one generation to learn about his father, Isaac.

In Genesis 26, Isaac was afraid, so he lied, deceiving Abimelech by leading him to believe Rebekah was his sister. Isaac's son Jacob, whose name means "deceiver," was afraid, so he lied and deceived his father and his brother

Esau. Many years later, Jacob was lied to and deceived by his father-in-law Laban.

This is the mystery of iniquity of lying and deception played out in Jacob's life. The full story can be found in Genesis 29.

Jacob worked seven years for Rachel's hand in marriage. On the wedding day, Laban deceived Jacob and gave Leah to him instead of Rachel. Jacob then worked another seven years of Rachel. After working a total of fourteen years, Jacob finally got Rachel, the love of his life. After twenty years of separation, Jacob was reconciled with his brother Esau, after he had an encounter with the angel of the Lord as is found in Genesis 32:24-30:

> *"Then Jacob was left alone; and a Man wrestled with him until the breaking of day. Now when He saw that He did not prevail against him, He touched the socket of his hip; and the socket of Jacob's hip was out of joint as He wrestled with him. And He said, 'Let Me go, for the day breaks.' But he said, 'I will not let You go unless You bless me!' So He said to him, 'What is your name?' He said, 'Jacob.' And He said, 'Your name shall no longer be called Jacob, but Israel; for you have struggled with God and with men, and have prevailed.' Then Jacob asked, saying, 'Tell me Your name, I pray.' And He said, 'Why is it that you ask about My name?' And He blessed him there. So Jacob called the name of the place Peniel: 'For I have seen God face to face, and my life is preserved.'"*

I love Jacob's words to his brother Esau in Genesis 33:10 NIV:

> *"For to see your face is like seeing the face of God, now that you have received me favorably."*

God changed Jacob's name, which meant deceiver, and gave him a new name, Israel, meaning prince with God. Praise the Lord! When our character is changed, He gives us a new name!

"...to him who overcomes I will give some of the hidden manna to eat. And I will give him a white stone, and on the stone a new name written which no one knows except him who receives it."

Revelations 2:17

As Ecclesiastes 3:8 states, there is a time for war and a time for peace. There will be times we must fight to defend our freedom. Because of war, innocent enlisted men and women have seen, and may have participated in, actions that violate their conscience and torment their emotional and mental wellbeing. Our enlisted men and women, who are just following orders, have suffered, but not because of their own sin. Often once discharged, they are flooded with painful memories of war. To then manage their memories and pain, they often find themselves relying on prescription or street drugs, to try to forget what they were apart of.

I share the following story of my dear friend Karen Chitty-Boe to show how amazing God is, how He intricately weaves our lives together for His kingdom and how He cares for us!

I met Karen through a mutual friend, Joyce Kahleh, who serves as Missions Director of Lakewood Church in Houston, Texas. Joyce learned of me while attending the Somebody Cares Summit. Pastor Doug Stringer had called me up to briefly share what the Lord was doing in Somebody Cares New England.

Several months later when Karen was traveling to New

England on business, Joyce gave her my contact information and encouraged her to come visit me while she was in the area. Karen did just that, and we have been "besties" ever since.

Karen loves the mission of Somebody Cares New England and has been a tremendous blessing to the ministry for many years. I shared with her the ministry of He Cares for Me and what God was doing in the ministry of healing and deliverance. She was so excited and said,

> "This is just what bible college students need to prepare them for the challenge of ministry. Healing Waters weekend will prepare them to be sent out with healing in their wings, equipped to minister to others with power and authority."

God is using Karen to sponsor bible college students for Healing Waters weekends. I thank God for her heart and willingness for God to use her to bring healing to so many.

Following is a testimony from one of the young men Karen sponsored, who is a Veteran and a student at the same college Karen graduated from.

A thankful Combat Veteran's "Healing Waters Weekend" testimony:

> "I just wanted to give God glory by sharing this testimony of healing and deliverance. Growing up, I went through a lot of abuse and my parents divorced. I moved to a bad neighborhood where I began to use crack cocaine and get into trouble. This lifestyle led me into a juvenile boot camp where I later joined the Marines and, the US Army, where I saw my fellow troops blown up and killed.

One night on a mission, I was hit by an explosion that cause my spirit to leave my body and I went into darkness. It was then I asked God if this was all I got to do with my life. I woke up to find my leg was almost blown off, and later in surgery, I lost a kidney, my gallbladder, some intestines, and had a traumatic brain injury. Hospitalized at Walter Reed Army Medical Center for a year, I became addicted to pain pills. After I retired, I became addicted to street drugs.

After four years of this, I decided I would be like the 22 other veterans who take their lives every two minutes. I made the choice to take my own life. After surviving a suicide attempt, I was put into a Veteran's hospital where a flood of emotions came to the surface. I got on my knees and began to pray for forgiveness for all that I had done. I witnessed a physical manifestation of Jesus Christ that day and gave my life to Him.

I still had much to be healed from when I was asked by Pastor Marlene Yeo to come to Healing Waters weekend. While I was there, they started off by washing my feet, and I could feel the presence of the Holy Spirit. Pastor Yeo guided me step by step when the Holy Spirit would bring to remembrance events I needed healing for. There was so much abuse, sexual sins, traumatic events on and off the battlefield, and a life of substance abuse.

At one point, the Holy Spirit brought an event to my mind and pastor Yeo led me through the process of renouncing the traumatic events from combat. This event had upset me for a long time, and I was deeply mentally wounded by it. I was crying and Pastor Yeo was praying for me. She rubbed anointing oil on my forehead and then on the back of my head at the base of my neck. When the anointing oil touched my neck my tears turned into hysterical laughter. I could not stop laughing.

She told me, "You are going through a deep inner healing." I haven't laughed like that since I was a child, and I could feel a heaviness being lifted off of me. I felt free, I felt joy, and I felt amazing! I renounced and took back authority from everything that the Holy Spirit brought to my mind; things that I had not thought about for many, many years. I left the church that day in victory, free for the first time in my life. I was taught to take back the authority from the enemy and started walking in the victory God has given me.

I went back to my dorm room, where later on that night, I felt a warm tingling feeling going through my injured shoulder and my tar filled lungs. God was still doing a healing in me, even when I was home. Healing Waters was an answer to my prayers, for the last four years since I became saved, I had been walking around, even after I gave my life to Jesus with deep wounds. After "Healing Waters", those wounds are now healed scars, stronger than they were before. I have now been trained on how to lead someone through this Biblical process of healing, and 1 look forward to seeing others walk in God's Victory.

During deliverance, when caring for one's soul, we always have to deal with some form of abuse from authority figures, both natural, such as parents, teacher, or police, and spiritual, such as priests, pastors or other church leaders.

Before looking at the story of David and Saul, referenced below, I recommend you read 1 Samuel 16 and 17. David's father Jesse didn't even acknowledge David as one of his sons when the prophet Samuel told him to bring all his sons. Once David was anointed as king, even his brothers were jealous of him. From David's life we see how complex and evil neglect and abuse is.

The verses you are about to read paint the picture of the emotional, mental and physical abuse that David experienced from King Saul, an authority figure in his life. To make things even more complicated, Saul functioned in the prophetic anointing when he was in the company of prophets. This complicates spiritual abuse. As the victim sees the abuser function in spiritual gifting, it messes with the victim's mind. It creates intense confusion for the victim, and causes them to question themselves and God. Why would God use someone so wrong to prophesy? We find the answer in Romans 11:29, the gift and the calling are without repentance. God doesn't remove spiritual gifts because of our character.

"Jonathan spoke well of David to Saul his father and said to him, "Let not the king do wrong to his servant David; he has not wronged you, and what he has done has benefited you greatly. He took his life in his hands when he killed the Philistine. The LORD won a great victory for all Israel, and you saw it and were glad. Why then would you do wrong to an innocent man like David by killing him for no reason? Saul listened to Jonathan and took this oath: "As surely as the LORD lives, David will not be put to death." So Jonathan called David and told him the whole conversation. He brought him to Saul, and David was with Saul as before. Once more war broke out, and David went out and fought the Philistines. He struck them with such force that they fled before him. But an evil spirit from the LORD came on Saul as he was sitting

in his house with his spear in his hand. While David was playing the lyre, Saul tried to pin him to the wall with his spear, but David eluded him as Saul drove the spear into the wall. That night David made good his escape. Saul sent men to David's house to watch it and to kill him in the morning. But Michal, David's wife, warned him, 'If you don't run for your life tonight, tomorrow you'll be killed.' So Michal let David down through a window, and he fled and escaped. Then Michal took an idol and laid it on the bed, covering it with a garment and putting some goats' hair at the head. When Saul sent the men to capture David, Michal said, 'He is ill.' Then Saul sent the men back to see David and told them, 'Bring him up to me in his bed so that I may kill him.' But when the men entered, there was the idol in the bed, and at the head was some goats' hair. Saul said to Michal, 'Why did you deceive me like this and send my enemy away so that he escaped?' Michal told him, 'He said to me, 'Let me get away. Why should I kill you?'' When David had fled and made his escape, he went to Samuel at Ramah and told him all that Saul had done to him. Then he and Samuel went to Naioth and stayed there. Word came to Saul: 'David is in Naioth at Ramah'; so he sent men to capture him. But when they saw a group of prophets prophesying, with Samuel standing there as their leader, the Spirit of God came on Saul's men, and they also prophesied. Saul was told about it, and he sent more men, and they prophesied too. Saul sent men a third time, and they also prophesied. Finally, he himself left for Ramah and went to the great cistern at Seku. And he asked, 'Where are Samuel and David?' 'Over in Naioth at Ramah,' they said. So Saul went to Naioth at Ramah. But the Spirit of God came even on him, and he walked along prophesying until he came to Naioth. He stripped off his garments, and he too prophesied in Samuel's presence. He lay na-

*ked all that day and all that night. This is why people
say, 'Is Saul also among the prophets?'"*

1 Samuel 19:4-24

When we have been abused, especially by authority figures, we respond one of three ways: flight, fight or freeze.

1) Flight away from everything and everyone who represents authority

We isolate and insulate to protect ourselves from further harm. Drop out of sight, school and work or depending on the level of abuse, people who choose the flight response often drop out of life and "Run Forest, run,"- and
keep running!

The flight response says, "Judge all authority figures as
evil and unjust and never trust anyone ever again; especially not God, He is the One that could have stopped the
abuse and didn't. The only one I can count on is me, myself
and I."

These precious victimized people stay as far away from
any form of relational church community life as they can.
They may drift in and out of a Sunday church service but
they would never have a relationship with anyone. They are
too afraid and think to themselves, "I will never get close to
anyone again. I cannot allow them to hurt me."

*"A man who isolates himself seeks his own desire;
He rages against all wise judgment."*

Proverbs 18:1

2) Fight, fight back, rebel and lead a revolution against
the "establishment."

You can let injustice catapult you into changing either

for the good or for the bad. Injustice was done against the blameless, innocent Son of God. He was abused for doing good. He led a revolution by living by the higher law of love, forgiving and blessing. He changed the world.

Peter resorted to using the sword when the religious leaders came to arrest Jesus in the Garden of Gethsemane, and the Lord rebuked him and said, "Those who live by the sword will die by the sword." I need to mention here that I am only referencing the wrong kind of revolution that breeds hate and that leads to violent actions whereby people destroy and harm themselves and others.

These precious victims become abusers who think that an "eye for an eye" is going to bring them justice. They believe that one bad deed deserves another. They breed the kind of rebellion that will bring them under judgment for themselves.

3) Freeze in place, emotionally and mentally in time and forever remain a subservient victim of abuse.

People who freeze simmer with rage just below the radar. They never allow themselves to feel or deal with the anger or let it motivate and move them forward into a different place in life.

The enemy knows that when we are submitted to God's sovereign authority, we are safe under the shadow of the Almighty. The devil is a strategist and a legalist whose plan is to get us out from under true godly authority, and victimize us by corrupt authority so that we are displaced from our place of authority in Christ.

The following chapter gives a beautiful example of submission to godly authority and the power it has to bring healing.

"And a certain centurion's servant, who was dear to him, was sick and ready to die. So when he heard about Jesus, he sent elders of the Jews to Him, pleading with Him to come and heal his servant. And when they came to Jesus, they begged Him earnestly, saying that the one for whom He should do this was deserving, 'for he loves our nation, and has built us a synagogue.' Then Jesus went with them. And when He was already not far from the house, the centurion sent friends to Him, saying to Him, 'Lord, do not trouble Yourself, for I am not worthy that You should enter under my roof. Therefore I did not even think myself worthy to come to You. But say the word, and my servant will be healed. For I also am a man placed under authority, having soldiers under me. And I say to one, "Go," and he goes; and to another, "Come," and he comes; and to my servant, "Do this," and he does it.' When Jesus heard these things, He marveled at him, and turned around and said to the crowd that followed Him, 'I say to you, I have not found such great faith, not even in Israel!' And those who were sent, returning to the house, found the servant well who had been sick. Therefore I did not even think myself worthy to come to You. But say the word, and my servant will be healed.'"

Luke 7:2-10

Notice the Centurion said, "I also am a man under authority." He was a Gentile, not a Jew, yet he could recognize and understand the authority of Jesus, "Say the word and my servant will be healed."

It takes faith to be under authority. The only way we have true godly authority is to be under godly authority.

No wonder the devil strikes and fights so hard to keep

us fearful and try to remove us out from under submission to authority.

We become a victim to our abuser. Once the abuse has successfully rewritten our DNA, we become compliant and subservient.

Scientists have discovered that the reticular formation is a part of the brain that is involved in actions such as the waking cycle and the sleeping cycle, and the filtering of relevant incoming stimuli to discriminate between irrelevant stimuli. The reticular formation is essential for governing some of the basic functions of higher organisms of the brain. The reticular holds the evolutionary history of a group of organisms, especially as depicted in a family tree. The dictionary definition of reticular formation: of or like a net; netlike, intricate; entangled.

As the wisdom of man has discovered the wisdom of God, this activation system in the brain is written about in Proverbs 23:7:

"As a man thinks in his heart so he is."

Whatever a man looks at, or thinks about will eventually manifest in his life because those things found entrance into his heart. It starts in the head, leaks into the heart and controls the decision making will. That is why it is so important not to look at anything that would cause your heart to be led into places that are dangerous to go.

Poet Ralph Waldo Emerson is quoted as saying,

"Sow a thought, reap an action; sow an action, reap a habit; sow a habit, reap a character; sow a character, reap a destiny."

However, long before Ralph Waldo Emerson, King David wrote in Psalm 101:1-4:

"I will sing of mercy and justice;
To You, O LORD, I will sing praises.
I will behave wisely in a perfect way.
Oh, when will You come to me?
I will walk within my house with a perfect heart.
I will set nothing wicked before my eyes;
I hate the work of those who fall away;
It shall not cling to me.
A perverse heart shall depart from me;
I will not know wickedness."

The reticular works in conjunction with what some call the law of attraction, but the Bible refers to as the law of sowing and reaping. Science has proven that whatever we give a lot of attention to, will become part of our lives. The theory of the law of attraction likens us to magnets that are constantly attracting the things we think about, as we previously read in Proverbs 32:7. This principle filters out information between what you are hearing and your subconscious mind. It is a gatekeeper and filter, depending on what you are looking at or are interested in.

We have both the conscious and the subconscious mind. The conscious receives 40 bits of data per second, the subconscious 40 billion bits of data per second. I find how God made us so fascinating as He is the Master of Science. For the purpose of gaining wisdom and understanding of the human need for healing and deliverance ministry I have included information about the Reticular. Some imaging studies have shown abnormal activity in the Reticular in people with chronic fatigue syndrome, indicating a high likelihood that damage to the reticular formation is responsible for the fatigue experienced with syndrome.

The chaotic, loose, and intricate form of organization of the Reticular is the mysterious area of the brain that seems to be at the crux of basic neurological and behavioral functions of the human body.

Traditionally, in the church, we only lay hands on the forehead, which is where the conscious part of the brain resides. Upon learning about the Reticular at the base of the spine, we started laying hands differently, placing one on the front and one on the back of the head. We invite the Creator of the mind to remove harmful data and restore the mind to function as it is intended to by the Original Designer.

Victimization isn't gender biased. It happens to both males and females. Think of the thousands of boys and girls who've been impacted because of Catholic priests or Christian leaders taking advantage of them. Will they ever escape the victim mindset? For many of those abused, if the Lord Jesus hasn't done a powerful transforming work in their lives, the abuse will repeat itself in the next generation. One of the devil's primary plans is to perpetuate victimization from one generation to the next.

Part of the problem with childhood sexual abuse is that the victim may not remember the experiences, they're trying to forget them. I know from experience that once God heals the pain, the memories are only just that- memories with no pain, no heartache and no more terror. Our emotions can only react, organize, or plan, they can't think. Emotions are involuntary responders to our circumstances.

Although our emotions can't think, they can be positive or negative in nature. A good emotion would be excitement, a bad reaction would be despair. A good emotion might be pleasure, and a bad response would be displeasure. A good emotion would be faith, and a bad response would be fear. There isn't any neutral ground when it comes to emotions. We may try to be unemotional, but even what we call an absence of emotion often reveals hidden emotional pain. We all manifest some level of voluntary or involuntary response to life's situations.

We need to understand how our emotions work because emotional responses often correspond to our personalities. Since emotions are reactors, they provide mental energy to whatever motivates us. When we think strongly about an issue, we generate strong feelings about the issue! For some of us it is abortion, for others it is politics, and for another it might be marriage, or war, or saving the whales. Our emotions trigger our will to act. We may act godly or ungodly. It depends in part on how healed we are from past wounds.

If our thinking is polluted by trauma, and we have developed wrong conclusions, it is possible that they will manifest in improper emotional behaviors, like various kinds of abuse, overeating, lying, domestic violence, alcohol, adultery, phobias, excessive spending, drugs or depression. A victim spirit, can exist on two different levels.

First, a "victim spirit" could refer to any one of a host of demonic spirits that are attracted to, and desire to attach themselves to, a person. Strongholds are established through lies that the victim believes. Then the victim acts out in accordance and gives credence to what they believe. After a period of time, the person then embraces a "victim identity." There is an unseen world of darkness filled with spirit beings just waiting and watching for opportunities to "kill, steal and destroy" lives (John 10:10).

When trauma occurs through any form of victimization, demons are ready to attach themselves to the wounded individual, which advances the cycle of events. The victim's fear, intimidation, and hopelessness are now supercharged by the demonic. This obviously causes troubling consequences. The terms used to describe demonic activity in an individual are:

- Demon obsession - to be mentally or emotionally obsessed by an evil spirit; i.e. confusion, hallucinations, fantasy, hearing voices in the mind, and paranoia.

- Demon oppression - the experience of feeling pressed down; (this can be in the mind, body, or emotions), like depression, lethargy, chronic fatigue syndrome, and suicidal thinking.

- Demon possession - Although the King James Version of the Bible uses the word possession, the original Greek word is "demonized." The word demonized describes a person vexed with a demon.

Secondly, a "victim spirit" is the human spirit of a person who's been violated in some way, intentionally or unintentionally, and has failed to process the experience properly. There is a specific mindset that a victim embraces that keeps the pattern of victimization reoccurring until it is broken. I'm not referring to everyone who has been abused, only those who continue to allow it to shape their lives. They have adopted a victim mindset and worldview by believing lies. Thus, they have developed predictable patterns of behavior. A victim can explain why it's right for things to be wrong, and they continue to allow a predator access to their life.

An example would be a woman who allows her husband to physically beat her year after year. In her mind, she has assumed lies that tell her she is the problem in the marriage and deserves beating. A predator is someone who preys on wounded and victimized people. In the above case, the predator would be the husband.

Three keys have to be in place to keep a person victimized:

1. A wrong mindset to program a lie about who we are
2. Meditating on and entertaining the lie, which then opens the door and invites demonic assistance in perpetuating the lie
3. A predator to assist the victimization

A demonic spirit of victimization has a voracious appetite. It must be fed to stay in place, If you want to get rid of a demon, starve it. Don't give it what it wants. It thrives on unforgiveness, resentment, judgments and self-condemnation. Many of us who have been victimized played little or no part in our victimization. This is especially true of innocent children. However, the enemy is shrewd. He will argue to an abused person that the pain they suffered was their fault. This keeps the victim paralyzed from ever leaving their circumstance and abuser.

Carol had been sexually abused. She attended a Healing Waters weekend having no idea of what to expect. Following is her testimony.

I was verbally forgiving those who had abused me physically, sexually and emotionally (since my early childhood). As I did, they were replaying like a video in my mind with details of each situation that occurred. With each painful memory, the enemy had heaped more shame, guilt and bondage on me, leaving the feeling more helpless and hopeless each time.

During the healing prayer following the ministry sessions on abuse the scales lifted from my eyes, and I could see how the enemy had a plan. From the beginning his plan, was to destroy my purpose and my destiny. As the chains were broken off and bondages broken, I could feel hope and renewed strength. I felt the Lord restoring to me all that the enemy had stolen from me. Most of all, I experienced God's love in a way I never had before. Since then, I have had many opportunities where I have seen and experienced restoration in several areas of my life. I give God all the glory and thank Him for birthing He Cares for Me ministry.

He Cares For Me

Living The Dream

Dr. Martin Luther King Jr. had a dream of freedom, not only for his people but for all people. God has a dream too, and His dream is that the Church would not just talk about Him as Father, but truly believe that He is our Father, and we are His family. The importance of community and living out our Christian faith within community has yet to be realized by most Christians. We live such independent, isolated and insulated secret lives. We have lost the art of praying, caring, and sharing our lives with one another.

Before knowing Christ, my world consisted of "us four and no more." It's an old expression that means my little corner of the world is all that matters, and if I mind my own business then everyone else should be minding theirs. My spin on it is, "don't bug me, and I won't bug you. Just don't touch my stuff and nobody gets hurt". The more refined and proper may say, "Just live and let live."

In my biological family, the relationships were far from life giving. They strained and drained life from me. The expression, "they suck the life right out of me," would describe it best. Once I gave the Lord residence in my heart, precedence in my mind, and preeminence in my daily life, He began to expand my heart, making room for all people, all ethnicities, all ages, and a special bond of love for those in the family of God. I am amazed by the grace God has given me to let others into what was once my own little world.

After a period of time, I became quite comfortable with

my new church family dynamic and settled into this new way of doing life with a community of believers that loved the Lord. With God as our Father, we were all brothers and sisters in Christ with the Bible as our standard for living life. As time went on, my immediate family got involved serving with me in our local church. We all enjoyed being with the family of God. Our closest and dearest friends became those in our church.

Many years later, I remember entering a season when my prayers began to change, and there was an aching in my heart for more of His presence. I felt desperate to know Him more. Even though what I had up until then was good, there was more the Lord had for me. Around that same time, my friend, Pastor Chad Waller, gave me a video produced by the sentinel group "Transform Nations." The Lord used that video to open my eyes to His heart for the world.

When the first video was produced in 1999, there were eight cities and nations documented that were experiencing God's power and presence. The transforming revival impacted government, and agriculture, as well as the social, economic and business sectors. Churches, families, and individuals were being radically changed by the power of God. There were tangible signs, wonders, and miracles for which there was no human explanation.

Since that first video, there have been numerous other DVDs produced that have captured the essence of what the Lord is doing globally in over 350 cities and nations. I encourage you to see for yourself at "http://www.glow-torch.org".

As God walked me through the journey of healing, I experienced freedom from the pain of my past. I began to see others' pain and brokenness, and I found myself being more concerned with others in distress because I was no longer consumed with the junk that was once in my trunk. Jesus had opened my prison door and sorted through all the confusion. He gave me understanding, forgiveness, and freedom. Now, I am able to offer what He has freely given to me to others.

Once the Lord captures your heart with His love and breaks it with what breaks His, you see the little, the least, the last, the lost, and the lonely through the lens of His compassion and mercy, instead of your own criticism and judgment.

I find when Christians are judgmental, critical and un-forgiving toward others, it is partly due to their own need for healing and freedom. You can only bear witness to and give to others the grace, mercy and freedom that you your-self have experienced.

"But you shall receive power when the Holy Spirit has come upon you: and you shall be witnesses to Me in Jerusalem, and in all Judea and Samaria, and to the end of the earth."

Acts 1:8

I personally have found that I must experience Christ in my own Jerusalem (my personal life where I live) before I can be His witness in Judea, Samaria, or the ends of the earth.

My prayer is that as you read this book, you will per-sonally experience the power of the Holy Spirit, and that God will use you mightily to bring deliverance and healing to others.

Godly relationships are meant to be life giving, encour-aging, strengthening and a blessing, not crushing, suffocat-ing, causing despondency, depression and death.

Professor Peter Cohen, in an article entitled, "The Opposite Of Addiction Is Not Sobriety. The Opposite Of Addiction Is Connection.", wrote, "Human beings have a natural and innate need to bond. When we're happy and healthy, we'll bond and connect with each other. If you're traumatized, isolated or beaten down by life, you will bond with something that will give you some sense of relief such as gambling, alcohol, sex or drugs."

A core part of addiction is about not being able to bear being present in your life.

Recovering addicts often say, as they rediscovered purpose, they rediscovered bonds and relationships and become functional in society. If you have a crisis in your life, it will be your meaningful relationships that will walk with you through to healing, but they cannot heal you!

Very few Americans have close friends. We have traded our connections for stuff and media, and the result is that we are a lonely society. The message you're not alone, we love you has to be at every level of how we respond to addicts. We should be singing love songs over them. The opposite of addiction, which causes isolation, shame and fear is not sobriety. The opposite of addiction is love, acceptance, forgiveness and connection.

"For He has not put the world to come, of which we speak, in subjection to angels. But one testified in a certain place, saying: 'What is man that You are mindful of him, Or the son of man that You take care of him? You have made him a little lower than the angels; You have crowned him with glory and honor, And set him over the works of Your hands. You have put all things in subjection under his feet.' For in that

He put all in subjection under him, He left nothing that is not put under him. But now we do not yet see all things put under him. But we see Jesus, who was made a little lower than the angels, for the suffering of death crowned with glory and honor, that He, by the grace of God, might taste death for everyone. For it was fitting for Him, for whom are all things and by whom are all things, in bringing many sons to glory, to make the captain of their salvation perfect through sufferings. For both He who sanctifies and those who are being sanctified are all of one, for which reason He is not ashamed to call them brethren, saying: 'I will declare Your name to My brethren; In the midst of the assembly I will sing praise to You.' And again: 'I will put My trust in Him.' And again: 'Here am I and the children whom God has given Me.' Inasmuch then as the children have partaken of flesh and blood, He Himself likewise shared in the same, that through death He might destroy him who had the power of death, that is, the devil, and release those who through fear of death were all their lifetime subject to bondage. For indeed He does not give aid to angels, but He does give aid to the seed of Abraham. Therefore, in all things He had to be made like His brethren, that He might be a merciful and faithful High Priest in things pertaining to God, to make propitiation for the sins of the people. For in that He Himself has suffered, being tempted, He is able to aid those who are tempted."

Hebrews 2:5-18

"So the LORD said to Cain, 'Why are you angry? And why has your countenance fallen? If you do well, will you not be accepted? And if you do not do well, sin lies at the door. And its desire is for you, but you should rule over it.'"

Genesis 4:6

"Stand fast therefore in the liberty by which Christ has made us free, and do not be entangled again with a yoke of bondage."

Galatians 1:5

Jesus is both the Lion and the Lamb. He came as the Lamb, lived like a Lion and died as Lamb. He has a lamb like nature- gentle, patient, kind, caring and meek. One of the best definitions of meekness is strength under control. Meekness does not mean weakness, or acting as a door-mat so that everyone can walk all over you. Meekness is seen in someone who is humble, teachable, and patient under suffering. It means the absence of any feelings of superiority, and it also means modest and lowly in spirit.

Humility is a lot like meekness. In humility, there is also the absence of any feelings of superiority or of being better than others. It is the act or posture of lowering oneself in relation to others in the absence of pride or self-assertion. People with humility esteem others better than themselves, and often put others' interests ahead of their own. It is an attitude one has towards oneself more than that of an attitude toward others.

Jesus also has a lion-like nature- strong, courageous, bold, fearless and wise.

While the lion represents the nature of Jesus Christ, the lamb represents the role that Jesus took when he submitted to the Father and become the sacrifice for our sin. In John 2:13, Jesus displays the passion and strength of a lion when he makes a whip and drives the money lenders from the Temple. This is the level of strength and courage that God has empowered us to have.

Jesus took on the role of the lamb when he was crucified on the cross. He humbled Himself to serve as the ultimate sacrifice for our sins. Jesus lived as a lion, but the lion became the lamb for a moment, so that we could have heaven for eternity. The lion (Jesus) became the lamb so that sheep (humanity) could live bold as a lion and gentle as a lamb.

Lions roar	Lambs bleat
Lions are confident and move wisely	Lambs are gentle and follow
Lions live to lead	Lambs live to be led

"Now as they observed the confidence of Peter and John and understood that they were uneducated and untrained men, they were amazed, and began to recognize them as having been with Jesus."

Acts 4:13

"Finally, be strong in the Lord and in the strength of His might. Put on the full armor of God, so that you will be able to stand firm against the schemes of the devil."

Ephesians 6:10-11

"If thou doest well, will not [thy countenance] look up (with confidence)? and if thou doest not well, sin lieth at the door; and unto thee [shall be] his desire, and thou shalt rule over him."

Genesis 4:7 DARBY

The priest said to them, "Go with confidence. The Lord will be with you on your mission."

Judges 18:6 NET

"For You, O my God, have told Your servant that You will build for him a house (a blessed posterity);

therefore Your servant has found courage and confidence to pray before You."

1 Chronicles 17:25 AMP

"For the Lord shall be your confidence, firm and strong, and shall keep your foot from being caught [in a trap or some hidden danger]."

Proverbs 3:26 AMP

"In the reverent and worshipful fear of the Lord there is strong, confidence and His children shall always have a place of refuge."

Proverbs 14:26

"The fear of man brings a snare, but whoever leans on, trusts in, and puts his confidence in the Lord is safe and set on high".

Proverbs 29:25

I can promise you, when you start walking in the confidence of true godly authority, you will be accused by others of being intimidating, controlling, dominating, self-righteous and overbearing. I think it's a riot when I am accused of these traits, when I know too well that as a child I was dominated, insecure and passive. I followed the crowd and blended in like a chameleon. Today, I can testify that I am no longer that person. The Lord has fashioned me into a bold, courageous, fearless leader.

"Now it happened when Sanballat, Tobiah, Geshem the Arab, and the rest of our enemies heard that I had rebuilt the wall, and that there were no breaks left in it (though at that time I had not hung the doors in the gates), that Sanballat and Geshem sent to me, saying, 'Come, let us meet together among the villages in the plain of Ono.' But they thought to do me harm. So I sent messengers to them, saying, 'I am doing a

great work, so that I cannot come down. Why should the work cease while I leave it and go down to you?' But they sent me this message four times, and I answered them in the same manner. Then Sanballat sent his servant to me as before, the fifth time, with an open letter in his hand. In it was written:

It is reported among the nations, and Geshem says, that you and the Jews plan to rebel; therefore, according to these rumors, you are rebuilding the wall, that you may be their king. And you have also appointed prophets to proclaim concerning you at Jerusalem, saying, 'There is a king in Judah!' Now these matters will be reported to the king. So come, therefore, and let us consult together. Then I sent to him, saying, 'No such things as you say are being done, but you invent them in your own heart.' For they all were trying to make us afraid, saying, 'Their hands will be weakened in the work, and it will not be done.' Now therefore, O God, strengthen my hands. Afterward I came to the house of Shemaiah the son of Delaiah, the son of Mehetabel, who was a secret informer; and he said, 'Let us meet together in the house of God, within the temple, and let us close the doors of the temple, for they are coming to kill you; indeed, at night they will come to kill you.' And I said, 'Should such a man as I flee? And who is there such as I who would go into the temple to save his life? I will not go in!' Then I perceived that God had not sent him at all, but that he pronounced this prophecy against me because Tobiah and Sanballat had hired him. For this reason he was hired, that I should be afraid and act that way and sin, so that they might have cause for an evil report, that they might reproach me. My God, remember Tobiah and Sanballat, according to these their works, and the prophetess Noadiah and the rest of the prophets who would have made me afraid."

Nehemiah 6: 1-14

The enemy of the kingdom of God would love nothing better that to get us off the assignment God has given us by getting our eyes off the prize, and getting our eyes on the people and the difficult challenges that we all MUST face. God wants to get us engaged in hand to hand combat. He wants us fighting the demons that accuse, maim, and want to destroy our testimony by getting us to "act that way" and sin.

This battle we are in, is over the Word of God in us. I am no one to be feared, and I have nothing that I should be a threat to the darkness. EXCEPT my testimony of who Christ is in me, and what He has done in my life. He is the conquering and soon coming King; Savior of my soul; He has delivered me, is delivering me, and making me whole. He is restoring to me all that the enemy had stolen. I have love, peace, joy, a bright future and a hope. Hope that on that day when I see Him face to face, I will hear, 'Well done daughter, welcome home, enter into the joy of the Lord and receive the reward of your labor done in My Name.'

> *"Then David said to the Philistine, 'You come to me with a sword, with a spear, and with a javelin. But I come to you in the name of the LORD of hosts, the God of the armies of Israel, whom you have defied. This day the LORD will deliver you into my hand, and I will strike you and take your head from you. And this day I will give the carcasses of the camp of the Philistines to the birds of the air and the wild beasts of the earth, that all the earth may know that there is a God in Israel. Then all this assembly shall know that the LORD does not save with sword and spear; for the battle is the LORD's, and He will give you into our hands.'"*
>
> 1 Samuel 17:45-47

I am not afraid of rejection or slander because my confidence rests in this: "I know in whom I have believed"

As Timothy 1:11-12 states:

"Whereunto, I am appointed a preacher, and an apostle, and a teacher of the Gentiles. For the which cause I also suffer these things: nevertheless I am not ashamed: for I know whom I have believed, and am persuaded that he is able to keep that which I have committed unto him against that day."

All I can say is, "Look what the Lord has done, and it is marvelous in our eyes" (and scary in some people's eyes). I have learned to rest in the finished work of the cross. I have learned that rest precedes rule and peace precedes power. As I rest in Him, I am learning to rule and reign with Him.

When visiting my friend Pastor Chad Waller's church many years ago, there was a guest speaker who, when praying for me, ministered prophetically saying, "I see angels all around you banging into each other, you keep them very busy trying to keep up with you, you go where angels fear to tread!" Chad and I had a good laugh. It is no secret; I like to move it, move it.

David received His confidence from being in the presence of God as he was tending his father's sheep. He fought, and won, against the lion and the bear. He learned confidence and authority over the creation that was entrusted to Adam in the Garden of Eden, and he was not afraid of the giant, for David knew of the delivering power of the Almighty God.

"And Saul said to David, 'You are not able to go against this Philistine to fight with him; for you are a youth,

and he a man of war from his youth.' But David said to Saul, 'Your servant used to keep his father's sheep, and when a lion or a bear came and took a lamb out of the flock, I went out after it and struck it, and delivered the lamb from its mouth; and when it arose against me, I caught it by its beard, and struck and killed it.'"

1 Samuel 17: 33-35

The following is an excerpt taken from the teaching "Overcoming the Accuser" by Rick Joyner. God has given us the authority to both close the gates of hell and open the doors of heaven. It is time for the Church to understand spiritual gates and do what we have been called to do- rule and reign with Him (in our garden) with influence, power and authority.

We are now entering the period when both will be fully opened. It is imperative that we are able to recognize each and use our authority to close one while opening another. Gates and doors are often localities where there are people. Spiritual influence of a city reaches far beyond the borders and boundaries. We must learn to distinguish spiritual boarders by their boundaries of influence. Just winning battles against darkness is not enough. Like Joshua at Ai, referring to Joshua 8:26 which goes on to say, "For Joshua did not draw back his hand, with which he stretched out the spear, until he had utterly destroyed all the inhabitants of Ai." If we fail to complete the job, our children will be confronted by the same deadly enemy.

Many in the church believe they can mix human and cultic philosophies into the fabric of their own life or the life of the church without serious consequences.

The Lord will not share His temple with idols. Judgment may not always come immediately, but it will come.

Roots of destructive heresies began years ago in the heart of those who compromised like Achan. Every Achan must be removed from the camp.

"But the children of Israel committed a trespass regarding the accursed things, for Achan the son of Carmi, the son of Zabdi, the son of Zerah, of the tribe of Judah, took of the accursed things; so the anger of the LORD burned against the children of Israel."

Joshua 7:1

"So the LORD said to Joshua: 'Get up! Why do you lie thus on your face? Israel has sinned, and they have also transgressed My covenant which I commanded them. For they have even taken some of the accursed things, and have both stolen and deceived; and they have also put it among their own stuff. Therefore the children of Israel could not stand before their enemies, but turned their backs before their enemies, because they have become doomed to destruction. Neither will I be with you anymore, unless you destroy the accursed from among you. Get up, sanctify the people, and say, "Sanctify yourselves for tomorrow, because thus says the LORD God of Israel: 'There is an accursed thing in your midst, O Israel; you cannot stand before your enemies until you take away the accursed thing from among you.'"

Joshua 7:10-13

"Now Joshua said to Achan, 'My son, I beg you, give glory to the LORD God of Israel, and make confession to Him, and tell me now what you have done; do not hide it from me. And Achan answered Joshua and said, "Indeed I have sinned against the LORD God of Israel, and this is what I have done: When I saw among the spoils a beautiful Babylonian garment,

two hundred shekels of silver, and a wedge of gold weighing fifty shekels, I coveted them and took them. And there they are, hidden in the earth in the midst of my tent, with the silver under it.'"

Joshua 7:19-21

Time to rise up, Church! It's time to be the end-time army of the Lord, clothed with His righteousness, filled with the power of the Holy Spirit, and forcefully advancing the kingdom together!

Every time a spiritual leader fails to take proper action against sin in the camp, they allow seeds to be sown for future defeat, division and destruction.

"Then he brought me back to the door of the temple; and there was water, flowing from under the threshold of the temple toward the east, for the front of the temple faced east; the water was flowing from under the right side of the temple, south of the altar. He brought me out by way of the north gate, and led me around on the outside to the outer gateway that faces east; and there was water, running out on the right side. And when the man went out to the east with the line in his hand, he measured one thousand cubits, and he brought me through the waters; the water came up to my ankles. Again he measured one thousand and brought me through the waters; the water came up to my knees. Again he measured one thousand and brought me through; the water came up to my waist. Again he measured one thousand, and it was a river that I could not cross; for the water was too deep, water in which one must swim, a river that could not be crossed. He said to me, 'Son of man, have you seen this?' Then he brought me and returned me to the bank of the river. When I returned, there, along the bank of the river, were very

many trees on one side and the other. Then he said to me: 'This water flows toward the eastern region, goes down into the valley, and enters the sea. When it reaches the sea, its waters are healed. And it shall be that every living thing that moves, wherever the rivers go, will live. There will be a very great multitude of fish, because these waters go there; for they will be healed, and everything will live wherever the river goes.'''

Ezekiel 47: 1-9

I am grateful to the Lord for true godly spiritual leaders who have been part of my healing journey, as well as an encouragement and example to me- Pastor Doug Stringer, Pastor Rafael Najem, Pastor Mike Servello, Sr., Pastor Michael Servello Jr., Pastor Jude Fouquier, Pastor Chad Waller and Pastor Dan Wermuth. They have loved me to life and as my dear friend Dr. Negiel Bigpond always says,

"You are like a river that gives me life and without you I cannot exist."

The course of our life is influenced by others. We have to be very selective about which voices we lend our ear to and what we give our eyes to. What we see and hear will determine the quality of our life. Paul warns the church in I Corinthians 4:14-16:

"I do not write these things to shame you, but as my beloved children I warn you. For though you might have ten thousand instructors in Christ, yet you do not have many fathers; for in Christ Jesus I have begotten you through the gospel. Therefore I urge you, imitate me."

We may have many instructors, but not many fathers in the Lord that we can imitate their life as they imitate

Christ.

It is critical that we align ourselves with people, mentors and ministries that are going in the same direction as we are obedient to the call of God on our lives. Fathers in the faith help prepare and equip us along our journey in the Lord. I learned that many years ago from one of the greatest mentors in my life Doug Stringer.

> "We need to be a people seeking consecration, asking and believing in faith for Him to do a work in us and get the rubbish out of our hearts. We must be sure to have proper perspectives, keep proper perceptions, be in proper alignments, agreements and associations and keep right attitudes."
> *- from Leadership Awakening, Doug Stringer*

We are all on a journey with Christ on the road of salvation that leads to eternal life. How we live out our faith EVERYDAY determines the quality of our lives and the quality of life for others. There will come a day when we will give an account for what we did with our 24 hours, along with the words we spoke, the deeds we did, the places we went, and, most importantly, the attitude and health of our own heart.

As ministers, we MUST honor our Father, submit to the Lordship of Christ, stay close to the cross in repentance, remain open and led by the Holy Spirit, search the Book of Life for wisdom and truth and stay on our knees in desperate prayer. We must war to stay pressed in. If we don't, then we risk the tragic fate of so many believers who started the race, but didn't finish well; those who waited for the Bridegroom but ran out of oil, as did the five foolish virgins in Matthew 25:1-3.

Live from the place of personal revival in the river (waters) of revival, and you will be a conduit of revival in the land! Jesus told the woman at the well in John 4:10:

"Jesus answered and said to her, 'If you knew the gift of God, and who it is who says to you, "Give Me a drink," you would have asked Him, and He would have given you living water."'

We must be willing to come to the waters, be washed in the waters, learn to drink from the waters, as well as lead others to where they can find the waters and show them how to drink.

"Ho! Everyone who thirsts, Come to the waters! "
Isaiah 55:1

I hope this book has encouraged you to seek the Lord for healing and deliverance in your own life, as well as for the sake of others. If you are ministered to by the book we would love to hear your testimony. If you are interested in registering for a Healing Waters weekend email: hcfmpsalm142@gmail.com.

It is time, Church, to be healed and to be His sent ones. He calls each one of us to be a witness and a minister. Many are in the valley of decision, and they need to see the power of the Lord in us, His church.

"But rise and stand on your feet; for I have appeared to you for this purpose, to make you a minister and a witness both of the things which you have seen and of the things which I will yet reveal to you. I will deliver you from the Jewish people, as well as from the Gentiles, to whom I now send you, to open their eyes, in order to turn them from darkness to light, and from the power of Satan to God, that they may receive forgiveness of sins and an inheritance among those who

are sanctified by faith in Me."

Acts 26: 16-18

Some get to travel to foreign lands like Paul did, some go back home and tell friends and family, some are sent into the marketplace of business, some are sent into the medical mission field to witness to medical professionals and some are sent into public service and education. Wherever He sends you, bring Him honor with your actions and your words and by the way you live your life.

"And when He got into the boat, he who had been demon-possessed begged Him that he might be with Him. However, Jesus did not permit him, but said to him, 'Go home to your friends, and tell them what great things the Lord has done for you, and how He has had compassion on you.' And he departed and began to proclaim in Decapolis all that Jesus had done for him; and all marveled."'

Mark 5:18-20

"After these things the Lord appointed seventy others also, and sent them two by two before His face into every city and place where He Himself was about to go. Then He said to them, 'The harvest truly is great, but the laborers are few; therefore pray the Lord of the harvest to send out laborers into His harvest. Go your way; behold, I send you out as lambs among wolves. Carry neither money bag, knapsack, nor sandals; and greet no one along the road. But whatever house you enter, first say, "Peace to this house." And if a son of peace is there, your peace will rest on it; if not, it will return to you. And remain in the same house, eating and drinking such things as they give, for the laborer is worthy of his wages. Do not go from house to house. Whatever city you enter, and they receive you, eat such things as are set before you. And

heal the sick there, and say to them, 'The kingdom of God has come near to you.' But whatever city you enter, and they do not receive you, go out into its streets and say, 'The very dust of your city which clings to us we wipe off against you. Nevertheless know this, that the kingdom of God has come near you.' But I say to you that it will be more tolerable in that Day for Sodom than for that city.'"

Luke 10:1-12

Share your testimony of His love that saves and His power that delivers. Do it with all your heart and with confidence, knowing that if the Lord sent you, then He is with you and if He is with you, He will accomplish His perfect will through you! We are not responsible to convince or to save others. We are commanded to love and to witness, and to rest in knowing that whatever the outcome may be, it is God's business.

"Jesus therefore answered and said to them, 'Do not murmur among yourselves. No one can come to Me unless the Father who sent Me draws him; and I will raise him up at the last day. It is written in the prophets, "And they shall all be taught by God." 'Therefore everyone who has heard and learned from the Father comes to Me.'"

John 6:43-44

"This is the word of the LORD to Zerubbabel:
'Not by might nor by power, but by My Spirit,' Says the LORD of hosts."

Zachariah 4:6

"Since, then, you have been raised with Christ, set your hearts on things above, where Christ is, seated at the right hand of God. Set your minds on things above, not on earthly things. For you died, and your

life is now hidden with Christ in God. When Christ, who is your life, appears, then you also will appear with him in glory. Put to death, therefore, whatever belongs to your earthly nature: sexual immorality, impurity, lust, evil desires and greed, which is idolatry. Because of these, the wrath of God is coming. You used to walk in these ways, in the life you once lived. But now you must also rid yourselves of all such things as these: anger, rage, malice, slander, and filthy language from your lips. Do not lie to each other, since you have taken off your old self with its practices and have put on the new self, which is being renewed in knowledge in the image of its Creator. Here there is no Gentile or Jew, circumcised or uncircumcised, barbarian, Scythian, slave or free, but Christ is all, and is in all. Therefore, as God's chosen people, holy and dearly loved, clothe yourselves with compassion, kindness, humility, gentleness and patience. Bear with each other and forgive one another if any of you has a grievance against someone. Forgive as the Lord forgave you. And over all these virtues put on love, which binds them all together in perfect unity. Let the peace of Christ rule in your hearts, since as members of one body you were called to peace. And be thankful. Let the message of Christ dwell among you richly as you teach and admonish one another with all wisdom through psalms, hymns, and songs from the Spirit, singing to God with gratitude in your hearts. And whatever you do, whether in word or deed, do it all in the name of the Lord Jesus, giving thanks to God the Father through him."

Colossians 3:1-25

I invite you to pray this simple prayer I have prayed for many years. "Come Holy Spirit. Heal me, fill me, and use me to show the world who You are through me and glorify Jesus!

Made in United States
North Haven, CT
01 May 2022

18784339R00087